ARE EVANGELICALS TRUE BORN AGAIN CHRISTIANS?

NYRON MEDINA

Are Evangelicals True Born Again Christians?
First Edition 2017
First written in November, 1997

All inquiries should be addressed to:

Thusia Seventh Day Adventist Church
Romain Lands, Lady Young Road,
Morvant,
Trinidad and Tobago
Telephone#: 1-868-625-0446

Unless otherwise indicated, Scripture quotations are from the King James Version of the Bible.

ISBN-13: 978-1976547003
ISBN-10: 1976547008

Front Cover Illustration by Nyron Medina

www.thusiasdaevangel.com

"Not everyone that saith unto me, Lord, Lord, shall enter into the kingdom of heaven; but he that doeth the will of my Father which is in heaven." Matthew 7:21

A Publication of Thusia Seventh Day Adventist Church
Printed in the United States of America

TABLE OF CONTENT

PREFACE

And he said unto me, Son of man, I send thee to the children of Israel, to a rebellious nation that hath rebelled against me: they and their fathers have transgressed against me, even unto this very day. For they are impudent children and stiffhearted. I do send thee unto them; and thou shalt say unto them, Thus saith the Lord God." Ezekiel 2:3,4

These words which God spoke to Ezekiel the prophet (in late June by the river Chebar) clearly represent the view of my mission to the "Christian" world and the world at large.

People are to be warned of a coming deluge of blood and fire (Revelation 18), especially the world of Evangelicals where there is theological anti-nomianism (anti-against, nomos-law). This world needs a baptism of true preaching and enlightenment concerning the Law of God and its relations to the converted man. It is because of the absence of the Law of God that this relatively new brand of Christianity has been sinking lower and lower down the scale of rational belief and morality.

The aim of this book is to illuminate all Evangelicals of the true facts about their religion. It is intended that they would see that their religion, (being born no earlier than the 1900's, with its roots stretching back into the nineteenth century), is a "hodge podge" combination of extreme excessiveness of Protestantism in its apostate form. That is, Evangelicalism was born in apostasy and was found in modern spiritualism combining most of the false doctrines of Protestantism when it was decaying.

It was spiritualism that gave birth to Evangelicalism and from the time of its birth down to the end of the twentieth century, it has progressively gotten worse. Its theology has gotten more anti-nominanistic. Its idea of the cross has devolved more repugnantly, and whatever remnants of ethics it inherited from the Holiness movement of the nineteenth century have well-nigh evaporated.

In this book I will show the Evangelicals the truth about their religion that they could escape for their lives from these doomed churches (Genesis 19:17).

At this time, I beseech you reader, if you have the courage and love of truth enough to read out this book, you shall gain a great blessing. There is a truth which will make you fit into the true position of God's people characterized in Revelation 14:12: "Here is the patience of the saints: here are they that keep the commandments of God and the faith of Jesus."

What would you do Mr. Evangelical, when you stand before God and recognize that you have been judged by the Law of God which you hated so much (James 2:8-12)? What would you do when you see your ministers condemned for teaching you to hate God's law and especially ***His precious Sabbath day*** (Matthew 5:17-19; Mark 2:27,28)? What would you do when you stand and see that "Blessed are they that do his commandments, that they may have right to the tree of life, and may enter in through the gates into the city." Revelation 22:14?

What would you do when you see that you are excluded with the "dogs" and "whosoever loveth and maketh a lie" (Revelation 22:15)? You will have **NO EXCUSE** because you have not only Moses and the prophets, but the voice of God's true remnant church (Revelation 12:17) warning you to "escape for thy life."

May you heed the warnings of this book after you have been enlightened, and may you receive true salvation from the grace of God and Jesus Christ. AMEN.

Elder Nyron Medina

Coal Mine, Sangre Grande

November, 1997

INTRODUCTION

Few people realize that not all "Christian" churches that name themselves after Christ are acceptable in God's sight. Not because one subscribes to a so-called "Christian" church, attend church services on Sunday, partake of church activities and pay a faithful tithe or maybe bring new people to church services will make that church God's true church.

Jesus himself gave a very relevant warning: "And as he sat upon the mount of Olives, the disciples came unto him privately, saying, Tell us, when shall these things be? and what shall be the sign of thy coming, and of the end of the world? And Jesus answered and said unto them, Take heed that no man deceive you.

"For many shall come in my name, saying, I am Christ; and shall deceive many." Matthew 24:3-5.

Here Jesus' first sign of his second coming is revelations of false Christianity deceiving many. This group comes in Jesus' name- they call themselves "Christian", they claim that Jesus is the true Christ, but they deceive many. Such a "Christian" church is false as Christ has presented. Paul, under the inspiration of the Spirit warned us of ministers of the Gospel, who are in fact Satan's ministers. "For such are false apostles, deceitful workers, transforming themselves into the apostles of Christ.

And no marvel, for Satan himself is transformed into an angel of light. Therefore it is no great thing if his ministers also be transformed as ministers of righteousness; whose end shall be according to their works." 2 Corinthians 11:13-15.

Of these ministers we are told: "Many will say to me in that day, Lord, Lord have we not prophesied in thy name? and in thy name have cast out devils? and in thy name done many wonderful works? And then will I profess unto them, I never knew you: depart from me, ye that work iniquity." Matthew 7:22,23. Here these ministers had preached a Gospel which made them think that they were prophesying in Jesus' name. They had done many wonderful works and miracles, chief of which was casting out devils. Such works were characterized by Christ as "iniquity" because they were deceiving many.

The wrong of these people was that they were transgressing the law of God. "Not everyone that sayeth unto me, Lord, Lord, shall enter into the kingdom of heaven; but he that doeth the will of my father which is in heaven." Matthew 7:21. God's will for humanity is clearly expressed in his law. Yet these miracles working ministers were teaching men to "...break one of these commandments..." Matthew 5:19, which is the Sabbath.

Solemn are the words contained in the following passages: "Then said one unto him, Lord, are there few that be saved? And he said unto them, strive to enter in at the strait gate: for many, I say unto you, will seek to enter in, and shall not be able. When once the master of all the house is risen up, and hath shut the door, and ye begin to stand without, and to knock at the door, saying Lord, Lord, open unto us; and he shall answer and say unto you, I know you not whence ye are: Then shall ye begin to say, We have eaten and drunk in thy presence, and thou hast taught us in our streets. But he shall say, I tell you, I know you not whence ye are; depart from me, all ye workers of iniquity. There shall be weeping and gnashing of teeth, when ye shall see Abraham, and Isaac, and Jacob, and all the prophets, in the kingdom of God and you yourselves thrust out." Luke 13:23-28.

How horrible it is to think of this, yet this is exactly what will happen to so many evangelicals because they were in a wrong religion- a religion that had a pretended Christ, a false Christ as evidenced by the teachings and practices of that religion. We are indeed to preach Christ and him crucified (1 Corinthians 1:23), but Christ does not come to us as a person in flesh, no, Christ said that he was the Truth (John 14:6). He comes to us as a doctrine: "Whosoever transgresseth, and abideth not in the doctrine of Christ, hath not God. He that abideth in the doctrine of Christ, he hath both the Father and Son." 2 John:9.

Thus it is absolutely necessary to have the right doctrine of Christ if one is to possess both Christ and the Father, so that if one has a false doctrine of Christ, one does not have the real Christ or the Father. Take for example, some of the teachings of Evangelicalism as they have presently devolved. Here is Benny Hinn in a message broadcast worldwide through the Trinity broadcasting network. He said:

*"God came from heaven, became a man, made man into little gods, went back to heaven as a man. He faces the Father as a man. I face devils as the son of God...,Quit your nonsense! What else are you? If you say, **I am**, you are saying I am part of Him, right? Is he God? Are you His offspring? Are you His children?* **You can't be human! You can't! You can't!** *God didn't give birth to flesh...you said, "Well, that's heresy." No, that's your crazy brain saying that."* Quoted from: Hank Hanegraaff, **Christianity in Crisis**, pp. 130-131.

Do you believe in this teaching? Is this not heresy? Would you say that Christ made us little gods? Should you designate yourself as "I am"? No certainly not! This is indeed heresy. This is an example of the false doctrines that are deceiving many and are destroying Evangelicals. Certainly to hold this doctrine is to transgress the law of God and to be without Christ and God.

Here is another example of Evangelicals. Mr. Kenneth Copeland is speaking of a prophecy which he said Christ told him:

"Don't be disturbed when people put you down and speak harshly and roughly to you. They spoke that way of me, should they not speak that way of you? The more you get to be like me, the more they are going to think that way of you. They crucified me for claiming that I was God but I hadn't claimed that I was God; I just claimed that I walked with Him and that He was in me. Hallelujah." **Ibid.**, pp. 137,138.

We are told that:

"...upon being questioned about this blasphemy, Copeland replied,"

"I didn't say Jesus <u>wasn't</u> God, I said He (Jesus) didn't <u>claim</u> to be God when he lived on the earth. Search the Gospels for yourself. If you do, you'll find what I say is true." **Ibid.**, p. 138.

Is this not clear enough to see how much Evangelicalism is deteriorating? And those Evangelicals who cling to this false form of Christianity which has taken up and combined all the extreme and heresy producing errors of the nineteenth century Holiness Movement, will further descend into crass spiritualism like the ancient anti-nomian, gnostic Christian sect of the second and third centuries.

How about the favourite of many Evangelicals- Mr. Morris Cerullo? He is God also-or, so he claims:

"Did you know that from the beginning of time the whole purpose of God was to reproduce Himself?...who are you? Come on, <u>who are you?</u> Come on, say it: 'Sons of God!' Come, say it! And what does work inside us, brother, is the manifestation of the expression of all that God is and all that God has. And when we stand up here, brother, you're not looking at Morris Cerulo, you're looking at God. You're looking at Jesus." **Ibid.**, p. 109.

This is New Age spiritualistic teaching. When one looks at the converted man one does not look at God or Jesus, one is looking at a child of God, a reflection of Christ, or at best, one in whom God dwells but certainly not God or Jesus. How about Mr. Price? Read what he said:

> *"Christ has redeemed us from the curse of the Law, that the blessing of Abraham might come upon us...How did God bless Abraham? With cattle, gold, manservants, maidservants, camels, and asses. Abraham was blessed materially."* **Ibid.**, p. 213.

Just as this man has forgotten that this blessing was "Justification by Faith" (Galatians 3:8,9,14), so we shall not forget to expose certain Evangelical doctrines to be false.

CHAPTER 1
THE ORIGIN OF THE EVANGELICALS

The Evangelicals arose out of decaying Methodism after their predecessor Seventh-day Adventists. Many scholarly literature have testified to the fact that Methodism arose at the time when German anti-nomianism and Calvinistic "particular predestination" had exhausted the spiritual sensibilities of the people. The longing for inner religion or "experimental religion" was met by Methodism which was the result of the Holy Club, set up by the Wesleys around 1725.

After Methodism had spread all over America and itself was decaying, Adventism arose out of it in the Millerite awakening of the early 1840's.

> "Seventh-day Adventists are heirs of the Wesleyan tradition in America...Millerites and Seventh-day Adventists furthermore, came into being at a time when John Wesley's American Methodist Movement so dominated American Protestantism..." **Spectrum** Vol. 25, No. 5 p. 26.

"...the most immediate and essential influence on Adventism has been the Wesleyan tradition." **Ibid.**, p. 48.

"It is long past time to emphasize that the Wesleyan heritage is one of Adventism's oldest, largest, and most deeply rooted trunks. An Adventist aware of its Methodist roots has a better chance of avoiding the contrary but equally disastrous outcomes of fundamentalism..." **Ibid.**, p. 38.

After Adventism had departed, Methodism descended into error and gave birth to an extreme erroneous "hodge podge" of churches known as the Holiness Movement. Read these evidences:

"Originating in the United States in the 1840's and 50's, this (the Holiness Movement) was an endeavour to preserve and propagate John Wesley's teaching on entire sanctification and Christian perfection... [There were] protests within the Methodist churches about the decline of discipline which resulted in the Wesleyan Methodist secession in 1843 and Free Methodist withdrawal in 1860. These two became the first denominations formally committed to Holiness... The increasing number of Holiness evangelists, many of whom were unsanctioned by their superiors, a flourishing independent press, and the growth of non-denominational Associations, gradually weakened the position of mainline Methodism in the Movement. By the 1880's the first independent Holiness denomination had begun to appear, and tensions between Methodism and the Holiness Associations

escalated. The gap between the two widened, as Methodist practice drifted steadily toward a sedate, middle-class American Protestantism, while the Holiness groups insisted they were practicing primitive Wesleyanism and were the true successors of Wesley in America." Walter A. Elwell, (Editor), **Evangelical Dictionary of Theology**, pp. 516,517.

The doctrines of the Holiness Movement were founded upon a dangerous "holy flesh" error of sanctification. This Movement itself was already an illegitimate child before it gave birth to an even sicklier child called Pentecostalism.

Observe what the general teaching of the Holiness Movement was.

"In the second [crisis], entire sanctification or full salvation, one is liberated from the flow in his moral nature that causes him to sin." **Ibid.**, p. 517.

"Those who sought to receive the "second blessing" were taught that each Christian needed to "tarry... for the promised baptism in the Holy Spirit; this would break the power of inbred sin and usher the believer into the spirit filled life... Spirit baptism brought "sinless perfection..." Holiness theology, with its belief is instantaneous purification from sin or spiritual empowerment..." Stanley M. Horton (Editor), **Systematic Theology**, pp. 11,12,13.

While we know that sinless perfection is achievable and will be achieved by God's people, and that, only after a prolonged struggle with

3

the world, the flesh and the devil, the Holiness Movement's ideas of the Holy Spirit with the aid of grace falling upon a person and at that instant he is sinlessly perfect or he is free from "inbred sin" amounted to a "holy flesh" heresy.

It is foolish to think that "sin in the flesh" goes with the reception of the Holy Spirit. The problem of sin starts in the heart, "For to be carnally minded is death...Because the carnal mind is enmity against God for it is not subject to the law of God: neither indeed can be. So then they that are in the flesh cannot please God." Romans 8:6-8. It is repentance and forgiveness of the sin of the heart that is needed, or the removal of the carnal mind, that there would be no perverted feelings in the flesh, or that the "body of sin" might be crucified. (See Acts 8:21,22; Romans 6:6). Nevertheless, it is out of this erroneous Holiness Movement that Evangelicalism or Pentecostalism as we know it today, arose.

> "The major milieu out of which Pentecostalism sprang was the Worldwide Holiness Movement, which had developed out of the nineteenth century American Methodism. Leaders in this movement were Phoebe Palmer and John Iwskip, who emphasized a "second blessing" crisis of sanctification through the "baptism in the Holy Spirit"." Walter A. Elwell (Editor), **Evangelical Dictionary of Theology**, p. 836.

But of this Evangelical or Pentecostal movement, the actual history of speaking in tongues is associated with its rise and distinction from the Holiness movement. Here are the real historical facts about the origin of tongues-speaking among Evangelicals.

> *"Although speaking in tongues had appeared in the nineteenth century in both England and America, it had never assumed the importance attributed to it by the later Pentecostals. For instance, glossolalia occurred in the 1883's under the ministry of Presbyterian Edward Irving in London, in the services of Mother Ann Lee's Shaker movement, and among Joseph Smith's Mormon followers in New York, Missouri and Utah. The Pentecostals, however, were the first to give doctrinal primacy to the practice."* **Ibid.**, p. 836.

But how did tongues-speaking develop among Evangelicals? We are told that Pentecostalism...

> *"...usually traces its roots to an outbreak of tongue speaking in Topeka, Kansas in 1901 under the leadership of Charles Fox Parham who formulated the basic Pentecostal doctrine of "initial evidence" after a student in his Bethel Bible School, Agnes Ozman, experienced glossolalia in January 1901."* **Ibid.**, pp. 835-836.

> *"Also hoping that they too would receive the power of the Spirit to quickly evangelize the world were the Kansas Holiness preacher Charles Fox Parham and his followers. Convinced by their own study of the book of Acts and influenced by Irvin and Sandford, Parham reported a remarkable revival at the Bethel Bible Study School in Topeka, Kansas in January 1901. Most of the students*

and Parham himself rejoiced at being baptized in the Spirit and speaking in tongues (i.e., xenolalia). Just as God had filled the 120 with the Holy Spirit on the Day of Pentecost, they too had received the promise (Acts 2:39). In fact, the "apostolic faith" of the New Testament Church had at last been fully restored. It followed then that Bennett Freeman Lawrence would name the first history of the Pentecostal movement The Apostolic Faith Restored (1916). Parham's distinctive theological contribution to the movement lies in his insistence that tongues represents the vital "Bible evidence" of the third work of grace: the baptism in the Holy Spirit, clearly illustrated in the pattern of chapters 2, 10 and 19 in Acts. In his **Voice Crying in the Wilderness** *(1902, 1910), Parham wrote that recipients were sealed as "the bride of Christ..."* Stanley M. Horton, **Systematic Theology**, pp. 16-17.

This is the first real instance that gave birth to modern Evangelicalism or Pentecostalism as we know it, but here is more that really caused the Movement to spread.

"Though Pentecostals recognize such sporadic instances of tongue-speaking and other charismatic phenomena throughout the christian era, they stress the special importance of the Azusa Street revival, which occurred in an abandoned African Methodist Episcopal church in downtown Los Angeles from 1906 to 1909 and which launched Pentecostalism as a worldwide Movement. The Azusa Street services were led by William J. Seymour, a black

Holiness preacher from Houston, Texas, and a student of Parham." Walter A. Elwell, **Evangelical Dictionary of Theology**, p. 836.

"The revival became a Pentecostal explosion when, in 1906, W. J. Seymour secured an old two-story frame building at 312 Azusa Street in Los Angeles, California. For about three years services ran almost continually, from ten in the morning to midnight. Many of those who received the Pentecostal baptism in the Holy Spirit there, scattered to spread the message. Many independent Pentecostal churches sprang up.," William W. Menzies and Stanley M Horton. **Bible Doctrines A Pentecostal Perspective,** p. 10.

Pentecostal churches are still springing up all over the world. But are they sound in teaching and practice? Observe how they were originally viewed.

"After 1906 Pentecostalism spread rapidly in the United States and around the world. Despite its origins in the Holiness Movement, the majority of Holiness leaders rejected Pentecostalism, and there were occasional charges of demon possessions and mental instability. Leaders of the older Holiness denominations rejected pentecostal teachings outright." Walter A. Elwell, **Evangelical Dictionary of Theology**, p. 837.

The aim of this book is to investigate some of the major teachings of the Evangelical/Pentecostal Movement. As I have shown before, when this Movement arose, it took up all the errors of the

Holiness Movement and it added to it, errors of its own. Put it this way; if I can scrape up all the evils and extremities of the Holiness teachings and put it into an old Pentecostal bottle, all that is left to do is to put additional erroneous teachings and, bingo, we will have what is called Evangelical teachings today.

> "Thus, when tongue-speaking occurred in Topeka in 1901, the only significant addition to the foregoing was to insist that tongue-speaking was the biblical evidence of receiving the Holy Spirit baptism. All the other teachings and practices of Pentecostalism were adopted whole cloth from the Holiness milieu in which it was born, including its style of worship, its hymnody and its basic theology." **Ibid.**, p. 836.

> "When the Pentecostal Movement began, a few years later, only the priority given to the gift of tongues distinguished it theologically from Holiness beliefs." Stanley M. Horton, **Systematic Theology**, pp. 15-16.

Thus Evangelicalism or Pentecostalism must be examined from the Bible to see if they teach the "thus saith the Lord". I can assure you readers that you shall not find this to be the case; instead you will find, coming from this Movement, an image of fanaticism, extremism and unsoundness of mind. You will observe how much of their teachings have been accepted at face value without close scrutiny or searching of the Bible.

In addition, you shall see glaring contradictions, forced inter-pretations and doctrines that actually deny the efficacious nature of Christ's sacrifice; salvation in sin and raw anti-nomianism that actually attacks God's holy nature. For example: If the "Righteousness of the Law" makes man self-righteous without Grace, and Grace only came with Christ, then before Christ came, God who gave the Law and demanded that men should obey it has caused men to be self-righteous because He did not send Grace. By implication, this means that God is not all-wise and loving.

.

CHAPTER 2
THE "SPEAKING IN TONGUES" HERESY

The Evangelical's or Pentecostal's doctrine of "speaking in tongues" as they call it, is the most central teaching of their faith. Indeed, it can be called the very foundation and origin of their religion.

As I have explained in the previous chapter, Evangelicalism was born in 1901 through the "speaking in tongues" phenomena that occurred in Topeka, Kansas under Charles Fox Parham and later in 1906-1909 in Azusa Street in the State of California.

My aim is to show that this phenomenon was a manifestation of modern "Christian spiritualism" under the influence of demons. The Holiness Movement, already an aberration from Methodism, and a propagator of a fanatical brand of entire sanctification, provided the Movement with "doctrines of devils" that Satan and his angels could have used in their miracle working powers.

Mr. Grider commenting on the Holiness Movement's ideas of sanctification said:

"For over 100 years in America's Holiness Movement, virtually all its authors have taught that the baptism with (or "of") the Holy Spirit is that instantaneous occurrence by which entire sanctification is wrought...This represents a change from John Wesley's view, however, he did not associate Pentecost with the second work of grace (entire sanctification), but rather with justification. He no doubt understood Pentecost to be associated with some kind of cleansing, according to his **Explanatory notes upon the New Testament** *at Matt. 3:11. Yet he did not identify the cleansing by its fires with the cleansing of entire sanctification"* J. Kenneth Grider, **Entire Sanctification**, p. 58.

And so, with the further drop in Christian doctrine in the Holiness Movement, the emphasis then moved towards the Supernatural, so that by 1901 a further all-time low came in the "speaking in tongues occurrence".

"The American Pentecostal Movement began on January 1, 1901, when a group of Bible students in Topeka, Kansas were filled with the Holy Spirit and spoke in tongues as the original Christians did on the day of Pentecost..." Compiled and Edited by David A. Womack, **Pentecostal Experience, The Writings of Donald Gee**, p. 11.

While these deluded Christians thought that they were reliving the day of Pentecost, their "speaking in tongues" was not in fact any language as that which the apostles spoke. The experience of these

Pentecostals was and has always been spiritualistic. The facts are, the Movement began in demonic spiritualism and has ever since that time grown in spiritualism.

A little search into the Bible will reveal that all Christians are not given the gift of tongues although all must have the Holy Spirit if they are to be true Christians. Paul tells us "But ye are not in the flesh, but in the Spirit, if so be that the Spirit of God dwell in you. Now if any man have not the Spirit of Christ, he is none of his." Romans 8:9.

Observe that without the Spirit dwelling in us we are not Christians. Also, in the following scriptures not all persons will receive the gift of tongues even though they have the Spirit of Christ. "And God hath set some in the church, first apostles, secondarily prophets, thirdly teachers, after that miracles, then gifts of healings, helps, governments, diversities of tongues. Are all apostles? Are all prophets? Are all teachers? Are all workers of miracles? Have all the gifts of healing? do all speak with tongues? do all interpret?" 1 Corinthians 12:28-30. Just as certainly as everyone in the church is not apostles or prophets, so one can infer from Paul's questions that not all in the church speak in tongues, although all must have the Spirit.

Despite this plain inference in the scriptures, Pentecostals still teach that all must speak in tongues as evidence of receiving the Holy Spirit. Observe:

"The third view of tongues as the evidence of being baptized in the Holy Spirit is the traditional Pentecostal position. Pentecostals commonly contend that speaking in tongues is always the initial physical evidence of this special experience. In fact, as J. R. Williams notes: "Pentecostals have laid particular stress on speaking in tongues as "initial evidence" of the baptism in the spirit ... Pentecostals believe their conclusion about tongues being the initial physical evidence of the baptism in the Holy Spirit is based on Scripture, especially the Book of Acts. In three cases where Luke records details of individuals experiencing being baptized in the Holy Spirit, speaking in tongues is clearly evident." Edited by Stanley M. Horton, **Systematic Theology**, pp. 439, 440.

"Pentecostals contend that speaking in tongues was the normal, expected experience of all New Testament believers who are baptized in the Holy Spirit. That is, the **primary activity** *consequent to the reception of the Holy Spirit was that of speaking in tongues."* **Ibid.**, p. 441.

It was the founder of Pentecostalism Charles Fox Parham that propagated this doctrine from the very beginning, although it was contrary to the scriptures (see 1 Corinthians 12:28-30.). In fact, it was this erroneous teaching that "all must speak in tongues as proof of receiving the Holy Spirit" that first led to the demonic workings causing Parham's students to speak in "tongues".

Observe Mr. Holdcroft's statement as he confirms this phenomenon:

"By the beginning of the 20th century, the stage had been set to respond to a pivotal event that would elevate Pentecostalism from a local and personal experience to an overall basic theological system. Such an event occurred on New Year's Day, 1901, in the Bethel Bible School of Topeka, Kansas. The students, numbering about 40, had been assigned by their principal, Rev. Charles Fox Parham, (1873-1929), a Holiness evangelist, to determine the Biblical evidence for the baptism in the Holy Spirit. They had concluded that tongues were the evidence, and the Pentecostal experience of a cold student, Miss Agnes N. Ozman (later Agnes La Berge), in the New Year's prayer meeting confirmed their conclusions. Other students received also, and classes were suspended while the entire school set forth to proclaim the new message." L. Thomas Holdcroft, **The Holy Spirit**, p. 104.

Thus the Pentecostal Movement began in doctrinal error, and this opened the way for demonic spiritualism to enter, dressed in Christian garments.

In 1 Corinthians 14, there are clear biblical expositions that explain what is speaking in tongues. However, we must understand that by tongues, "languages" are meant and not the form of incoherent babblings or mutterings that occur in the Evangelical Movement which they call tongues. The book of Acts tells us: "And when the day of Pentecost was fully come, they were all with one accord in one place. And suddenly there came a sound from heaven as of a rushing mighty wind, and it filled all the house where they were sitting. And there appeared unto them cloven tongues like as of fire, and it sat upon each of them. And they were all filled with the Holy Ghost, and began to speak with other tongues, as the Spirit gave them utterance." Acts 2:1-4.

According to the following verses, these tongues were various languages. "Now when this was noised abroad, the multitude came together, and were confounded, because that every man heard them spake in his own language. And they were all amazed and marvelled, saying one to another, Behold, are not all these which speak Galileans? And how hear we every man in his own tongue, wherein we were born?" Acts 2:6-8. Thus the disciples spoke the actual recognizable languages of different nations, but they did not understand the languages since they never learned them, but they understood what they were speaking, they were speaking "...the wonderful works of God." Acts 2:11.

It was the hearers of the apostles that understood the various languages according to their nationalities. What were their nationalities? According to Acts 2:9-11, there were Parthians, Medes, Elamites, Mesopotamians, Judeans, Cappadocians, Pontians, Asians, Phrygians, Pamphylians, Egyptians, Libyans, Cyrenians, Romans, Cretians and Arabians. Thus the Bible records some of the different languages the apostles spoke through the miraculous endowment of the Holy Spirit.

We also observe that the disciples were of "one accord" (Acts 2:1) when this miracle happened. But this is not the case in Pentecostal meetings when they experience their "false" tongues. Holy lives and unity are lacking in their members, and the least thing they have is unity.

I remember an incident which occurred in my early Christian existence which explains adequately what I am speaking about. There was a teenage girl, who was brawlish and always looking to fight with whomsoever she disagrees. One night, when the Church of God had a crusade in the Prizgar Lands area, she attended one of their meetings. I was also present at that meeting and saw all that transpired.

After the pastor had finished preaching, the music band had begun to play catchy songs to which the congregation was swaying and dancing. The pastor himself was speaking in "tongues" as they called it. He then raised his right hand and moved it horizontally from right to left loudly calling upon the dancing congregation to speak in tongues. As he moved his hand from right to left, the people in that order began to speak in "tongues" with great noises and some of them fell to the ground.

The particular unconverted girl fell to the ground speaking in tongues so that even her clothes raised up, someone then covered her with a white cloth. She spoke in "tongues" more than anyone else that night; while the others had finished she was still on the ground beating up, occasionally rolling from side to side and speaking in "tongues".

Later she left to return home. The next day, however, my friends and I saw her in her usual immoral behaviour, using obscene language. Now this is indeed contrary to the bible. The disciples had to fast and pray ten days in the upper room to receive the Holy Spirit to have such an experience so as to render them capable of starting the post-cross church (Acts 1:14), yet this unconverted girl in no time, without self-denial and any form of experience of holiness spoke in even more "tongues", and for a longer duration of time than all the other members of that particular church. Surely this is proof that the whole thing is unscriptural.

In these Pentecostal churches, the emphasis of the girls' dresses is to seduce the punk boys - woman hunters, rather than to appear before the presence of a holy God. These girls dress half naked and are the most vociferous in "speaking in tongues". When the disciples spoke in tongues on the day of Pentecost we are told that among the on-lookers, "Others mocking said, These men are full of new wine." Acts. 2:13. But these mockers said that because of how the disciples sounded in different languages, not because they fell on the ground and beat up as if struck by lightning, yet all these things occur in Pentecostal assemblies and these people are so blinded that they cannot even see that their behaviour is unscriptural.

Here is another of my personal experiences to illustrate. One night, I attended an Open Bible Standard Church on the Eastern Main Road, Laventille. That night many members were speaking in "tongues" to loud soul music. Facing the direction of north to the pulpit, to the left side about six benches from the pulpit, was a young woman, probably in her twenties. She was at the end of the bench close to the concrete wall of the church building. I was about four benches behind her on the left hand side of the church close to the wall. Hence I could have seen her clearly. The poor deluded girl was standing with her both hands upraised supposedly praising God. She was speaking in "tongues", then she began to sway more to the left of the concrete wall as if falling. Suddenly, she began to jump up and down, and this time she over did it and hit her head on the left side of the concrete wall as she fell to the ground. There was a loud noise as her head struck against the wall which attracted the attention of others nearby. Then she was on the ground beating up, her clothes were raised up and her underwear was showing. Some women quickly rushed and covered her with a piece of white cloth. After that, the poor girl had a terrible headache.

Now, I ask the question, is all this glorifying to God? Where is the scriptural parallel to justify this madness? Evangelicals like to quote Acts 10:44-48 to justify their speaking in tongues, but a brief look at these scriptures does not raise claim that **everyone** must speak in tongues as proof of reception of the Holy Spirit.

The miracle was meant especially for the Jews who had racial and sceptical problems about God accepting the believing Gentiles as His people. Observe, "While Peter yet spake these words, the Holy Ghost fell on all them which heard the word. And they of the circumcision [the

Jews] which believed were astonished, as many as came with Peter, because that on the Gentiles also was poured out the gift of the Holy Ghost. For they heard them speak with tongues, and magnify God. Then answered Peter, can any man forbid water, that these should not be baptized, which had received the Holy Ghost as well as we? And he commanded them to be baptized in the name of the Lord. Then prayed they him to tarry certain days." Acts 10:44-48.

The scripture is plain. God first had to show Peter by vision that he "... should not call any man common or unclean." Acts 10:28, as was the custom of the Jews, and so the miracle of Gentiles speaking in different languages was to prove to Peter and his Jewish friends that God converted or justified the Gentiles just as the Jews which believed; this is why Peter could now recommend water baptism for the Gentiles. But the Gentiles that believed spoke real languages that Peter may not have understood, but at least would have recalled the same tongues being spoken on the day of Pentecost.

Also, there are no records of the Gentiles jumping up and down, falling down on the ground and beating up as Pentecostals do; certainly, nobody's nakedness was revealed before the Lord.

Acts 19:1-7 is another text which is cited by Pentecostals for their "speaking in tongues". It reads: "And it came to pass, that, while Apollos was at Corinth, Paul having passed through the upper coasts came to Ephesus: and finding certain disciples, He said unto them, Have ye received the Holy Ghost since ye believed? And they said unto him, We have not so much as heard whether there be any Holy Ghost. And he said unto them, Unto what then were ye baptized? And they said, Unto John's baptism. Then said Paul, John verily baptised with the baptism of repentance, saying unto the people, that they should believe on him which should come after him, that is, on Christ Jesus. When they heard this, they were baptized in the name of the Lord Jesus. And when Paul had laid his hands upon them, the Holy Ghost came on them; and they spake with tongues, and prophesied. And all the men were about twelve." Acts 19:1-7.

Now how do we interpret this text? 1 Corinthians 14:22 is the answer. It says: "Wherefore tongues are for a sign, not to them that believe, but to them that believe not..." Apparently this incident was to encourage the men that Paul baptized that God had accepted them by giving them His Spirit, but this does not always occur, and nevertheless, these men spoke in real languages, not incoherent babbling like Evangelicals.

In 1 Corinthians 14 one would see this phrase "unknown tongue" in a number of verses; however, the word "unknown" is in italic style indicating that it is a supplied word and is not in the original Greek text. So, 1 Corinthians 14 says nothing about an "unknown" tongue as some Evangelicals like to cite. Rather, the whole chapter is a rebuke for Pentecostals and shows them up for what they really are- a counterfeit, a satanic delusion in Christian garbs.

It is not in place here to quote the whole chapter; however, you may read the whole chapter. I shall comment upon just a few scriptures.

CHAPTER 3
SPEAKING IN TONGUES IS NOT TRULY A LANGUAGE

We are now embarking on explaining some of the verses in 1 Corinthians 14 which adequately explain the question of speaking in tongues. It will be seen from these verses, that the manifestation that occurs in Pentecostalism, (upon which they are founded), is not the tongue speaking of the Bible. This religion is a new brand of Christianity unheard of before the 1900s; it is Christian spiritualism made up of most of the god-forsaken heresies of the last half of the nineteenth century. Now let us look at the scriptures.

"For he that speaketh in an unknown tongue speaketh not unto men, but unto God: for no man understandeth him; howbeit in the spirit he speaketh mysteries." 1 Corinthians 14:2. First of all, the word "unknown" describing tongue in the KJV is not in the original Greek, it is a supplied word. The phrase should be "...he that speaketh in a tongue..." and this is exactly the way we shall present it from henceforth; we will leave out the word "unknown".

Anyhow, Evangelicals love to quote the above text to justify what they call speaking in "tongues". They usually say that people cannot understand the "tongues" they speak because they are not speaking to men but unto God. However, the facts are, they cannot be understood, because what they are speaking is not any language at all. A little reading of the scriptures further on will confirm this.

"He that speaketh in a tongue edifieth himself; but he that prophesieth edifieth the church. I would that ye all spake with tongues, but rather ye prophesied: for greater is he that prophesieth than he that speaketh with tongues, except he interpret, that the church may receive edifying." 1 Corinthians 14:4,5.

Here Paul is saying that he would rather see church members prophesying than speaking with tongues, and that one prophesying is greater than one speaking with tongues, except that the one who speaks with tongues translate the language so that people in the church can understand and be edified.

But Evangelicals do not do this. No, no one understands what they are saying, but Paul continues: "Now, brethren, if I come unto you speaking with tongues, what shall I profit you, except I shall speak to you, either by revelation, or by knowledge, or by prophesying, or by doctrine." 1 Corinthians 14:6. This shows that no one in these "tongue speaking" churches profit anything, because they achieve no revelation, no knowledge, no prophesy or doctrine from the "speaking in tongues".

Paul continues: "So likewise ye, except ye utter by the tongue words easy to be understood, how shall it be known what is spoken? for ye shall speak into the air. There are, it may be, so many kinds of voices in the world, and none of them is without signification. Therefore if I know not the meaning of the voice, I shall be unto him that speaketh a barbarian, and he that speaketh shall be a barbarian unto me." 1 Corinthians 14:9-11. From the above words of Paul, it is evident that "tongue speakers" in Pentecostalism speak "into the air", and make "barbarians" out of each other. Even though some of them claim to interpret their "tongues", they are simply lying and practicing deception, because what they speak is no language at all, and it does not have the feature of a language.

Again, Paul speaks: "Wherefore let him that speaketh in a tongue pray that he may interpret." 1 Corinthians 14:13.

Did you read that Mr. Evangelical? Translate it or shut up! Again: "For if I pray in a tongue, my spirit prayeth, but my understanding is unfruitful. What is it then? I will pray with the spirit, and I will pray with the understanding also." 1 Corinthians 14:14,15. Whenever you are praying in "tongues" Mr. Evangelical, you may have an experience, but as Paul says, if you have no understanding of what you are saying, you know that it is not a manifestation of the gift of tongues by the spirit, it is a delusion of the devil. Stop it immediately, cease from that spiritualism, and confess that work of iniquity to God for forgiveness. Paul speaks: "I thank my God, I speak with tongues more than ye all: Yet in the church I had rather speak five words with my understanding, that by my voice I might teach others also, than ten thousand words in a tongue." 1 Corinthians 14:18,19.

Evangelicals do the complete opposite, and what Paul further explains is true of them also. "If therefore the whole church be come together into one place, and shall spake with tongues, and there come in those that are unlearned, or unbelievers, will they not say that ye are mad?" 1 Corinthians 14:23. This is exactly what happens all the time, thus Evangelicals do not speak in tongues the biblical way. "If any man speak in a tongue, let it be by two, or the most three, and that by course; and let one interpret. But if there be no interpreter, let him keep silence in the church; and let him speak to himself, and to God." 1 Corinthians 14:27,28.

Dear Mr. Evangelical, according to Paul, it is better that you shut up, sit at the feet of Jesus and learn. "For God is not the author of confusion, but of peace, as in all the churches of the saints." 1 Corinthians 14:33.

Why does the author present so much material on the speaking in tongues issue? It is because this is the foundation of Pentecostalism or Evangelicalism. They were born in 1901 in "speaking in tongues". This became their major doctrine, they spread all over the world on the basis of this doctrine, so if it falls, the major cause for their existence is destroyed and ultimately they have no further reason to exist. There are so many things about this speaking in tongues issue that need to be revealed, that this is hardly the place to accommodate all that revelation. Nevertheless, we shall look into a few more facets of this "tongue speaking" issue as a warning to Evangelicals to give it up and escape the baleful results of this form of Christian spiritualism. Let us take a look at the explanation of Mr. Rice:

> *"The idea that "speaking in tongues" meant some ecstatic jumble of words, not a regular language, or whether in ecstasy or not, a language known only to God-that idea came from secular literature based on the tongues of almost all heathen religions! That idea is not ever taught in the Bible."* John R. Rice, **The Charismatic Movement**, p. 28.

Mr. Rice quotes from a book in his book:

> *"In non-christian religions – Tongues occupied a significant place in ancient Greek religion. The seeress at Delphi, not far from Corinth, spoke in tongues. According to Plutarch (A.D. 44 – 117), interpreters were kept in attendance to explain her incoherent utterances. Many scholars have stated that tongues were experienced in the mystery religions (Osiris, Mithra, Eleusinian, Dionysian, and Orphic cults). Some have concluded that the unintelligible lists of "words" in the "magical papyri" and in certain gnostic "prayers" are records of ecstatic utterances. About A.D 180 Celus reported ecstatic utterances among the Gnostic. Lucian of Samosata (A.D 120 – 198) described tongues speaking as it was practiced by the devotees of the Syrian goddess, Juno. Today, shamans (witch doctors, priests, or medicine men) in Haiti, Greenland, Micronesia, and countries of Africa, Australia, Asia, and North and South America speak in tongues. Several groups use*

*drugs to aid in inducing the ecstatic stare and utterances. Voodoo practitioners speak in tongues. Buddhist and Shinto priests have been heard speaking in tongues. Moslems have spoken in tongues, and an ancient tradition even reports that Mohammed himself spoke in tongues. According to his own account, after his ecstatic experiences he found it difficult to return to "logical and intelligible speech ..." Extra biblical records are quite explicit with regard to unintelligible ecstatic utterances prior to the Christian era. As early as 1100 B.C. an Egyptian, Wen-Amon, recorded an incident when a young man in Canaan, seemingly "inspired" by his god, behaved strangely and spoke ecstatically all one night ... In three of Plato's dialogues he makes references to religious ecstatic speech. He discusses prophetic "madness" as a departure from one's normal senses. He cites the utterances of the prophetess at Delphi, the priestess at Dodona, and the Sibyl as examples of such madness or ecstasy. Only when those women were "out of their senses" that is, when their speech was unintelligible were their utterances considered significant. He also describes the incomprehensible speech of certain diviners whose utterances were expounded by an attendant prophet or interpreter...In the **Aeneid** Virgil describes the sibylline priestess on the island of Delos who in ecstatic state, spoke obscurely and unintelligibly. Such utterances were considered the result of some type of divine inspiration, and when "interpreted" by a priest or prophet they were considered divine oracles...It is apparent that tongues speaking occurred in pagan cultures prior to the day of Pentecost. Martin concludes that* *tongues have appeared in varying circumstances among different peoples, and in various periods of history. They have even appeared "outside the area of strictly religious phenomenon," and therefore, "no claim may be made for glossolalia as an exclusively Christian demonstration..." Tongue speaking occurs among anti-christian spiritistic mediums."* **Ibid.**, pp. 29-30.

Pentecostals, this then is a call for you to take warning and re-investigate your speaking in "tongues" and the foundations of your religion. Obviously, it is one with the unconverted false religions. Your tongues speaking is not really a language after all, but unintelligible jabbering as has been present in all ancient pagan religions.

Again:

"In extra biblical literature this word [glossolalia] was used to describe the "inspired" utterances of diviners. Moulton and Milligan cite three occurrences of the word in Vettius Valens where it designates irrational or unintelligible speech. It is stated that the speakers' minds had "fallen away", they were overcome with "madness," and they spoke in "ecstasy". Apoptheggomai was almost a technical term for describing the speech of oracle-givers, diviners, prophets, exorcists, ecstatics, and other "inspired" person." **Ibid.**, p. 32.

To Evangelicals I can say:

"It is wrong to put the heathen interpretation on the term "tongue" in the Bible. When a Delphi oracle in Greece talked in tongues, or when Mohammed, the founder of the Muslim religion talked in tongues, or when a witch doctor talks in tongues, that is not what God gave in bible times ..." Ibid., p.35.

What about Charles Fox Parham's "initial evidence" of the baptism of the Holy Spirit?

"But here, as we consider the pouring out of the Spirit at Pentecost, we see there is not a shred of evidence that the disciples regarded speaking in foreign tongues as the "initial evidence of the baptism of the Holy Ghost." It was never promised; it was never described that way on the occasion itself. Paul said nothing like that when he discussed the tongues later with the people at Corinth. That is a human, unjustified fabrication." **Ibid.**, p. 42.

What about a person inducing his own "tongues" speaking? This never happened with the apostles, but it happened when fraud and demon influence is around. Mr. Rice quotes an admission by a Mr. Sherrill:

"I had a sudden, violent reaction. It centred chiefly on tongues: I became suspicious that I was generating the whole thing. Indeed I often did mouth nonsense syllables in an effort to start the flow of prayer-in-tongues. But sometimes the easy, effortless flow never came. I'd be left listening to the sound of my own foolishness. It was

obvious to me that the Holy Spirit was no part of these noises. The ridiculousness of it would sweep over me and from there it was not far to wondering if the Holy Spirit had ever been a part of tongues." **Ibid.,** p. 108.

This man at least became finally realistic and honest to himself, but how many Evangelicals do not? Mr. Rice says:

"But many times we can be sure that the talking in tongues becomes a deliberate fraud. One by practice "grows" "fluent", as Pentecostalists themselves say." **Ibid.,** p. 145.

What do they say? Mr. Rice quotes an Evangelical who showed him how to speak in tongues.

"I knew a godly, soul-winning preacher, a good man. He told me that he had been active in the Pentecostal churches and had talked in tongues. He said, "I will show you how," and he cut loose in a Jabber and smiled at me. In other words, he was saying that he could imitate and put on the kind of show that people expected in the Pentecostal service and he had done it himself as a Pentecostalist." **Ibid.,** p. 145.

Of course we do not agree with Mr. Rice's description of the preacher as "godly" or "good". Whether a person fakes "tongue" speaking or whether it happens from evil spirits all are devilish.

> *"If Mormons can find themselves talking in tongues after similar rigmaroles, then it is probably no more from God for a Pentecostal to learn the same thing. If an unsaved Catholic, or a modernist professor in a university, or heathen American Indians, or original heathen Hawaiian leaders, or if priestesses of the Delphian Oracle in ancient Greece can bring themselves to talk in tongues, then it is not necessarily true that tongues are from God and people find it easy to convince themselves and to reach the state which they think is proper if they work hard enough at it and begin to jabber in what they think is a heavenly language."* **Ibid.**, p. 142.

Lest we forget that ancient pagans spoke the same jabber Pentecostals call "tongues" under the influence of evil spirits, let us look again at the facts.

> *"That tongues can be and are counterfeited by demon spirits is evidenced by the fact that spiritistic mediums, Muslim dervishes, and Indian fakirs speak in tongues. It must be remembered by those who try to make tongues a badge of spirituality or a status symbol of saints who have attained the height of spiritual experience, that speaking in tongues and their interpretation are not peculiar to the Christian church but are common in ancient pagan religions and in spiritism both ancient and modern. The very phrase "to speak with tongues" (Greek glossais lalein...) was not invented by New Testament writers, but borrowed from the ordinary speech of pagan. Plato's attitude towards the enthusiastic ecstasies of the ancient soothsayer (mantis, diviner) recalls the*

Apostle Paul's attitude towards glossolalia among the Corinthian believers. Virgil graphically describes the ancient pagan prophetess "speaking with tongues". He depicts her dishevelled hair, her panting breast, her change of color, and her apparent increase in stature as the god (demon) came upon her and filled her with his supernatural afflatus. Then her voice loses its mortal ring as the god (demon) speaks through her, as in ancient and modern necromancy (spiritism). Phenomena of this type are common among savages and pagan peoples of lower culture. Ecstatic utterances interpreted by a person in a sane state of mind have been verified. In the Sandwich Islands, for example, the god Oro gave his oracles through a priest who ceased to act or speak as a voluntary agent, but with his limbs convulsed, his features distorted and terrific, his eyes wild and strained, would roll on the ground foaming at the mouth, and reveal the will of the god in shrill cries and sounds violent and indistinct, which the attending priests duly interpreted the people." **Ibid.**, pp. 136-137.

Also, this demonic influence under the name of speaking in tongues cannot help but to bring instability and mental sickness to the minds of those fully influenced by it.

"The fact that nonreligious tongues speaking often occurs in association with certain mental illness is well documented. Psychiatrists have reported it in association with schizophrenia, neurosis, and psychosis. Probably all psychiatrists and psychologists are aware of the possibility of psychic damage

resulting from tongue speaking ... It was reported that following the extended tongues meeting held by Aimee Semple Mc Pherson, founder of the Church of the Foursquare Gospel, mental institutions in the area of her meetings were overburdened. The Episcopalian church financed a study commission which concluded that tongues are "not per se a religious phenomenon" and may appear among those "who are suffering from mental disorders as schizophrenia and hysteria". ...tongues speaking occur among anti-christian spiritistic mediums. Contrary to popular belief among tongues speakers, a few years ago the European Pentecostal Conference admitted that "tongues might occur apart from the Spirit's action." ...Even Pentecostal authors grant that there are cases where demonic influence is apparently responsible for tongues utterances." **Ibid.**, p. 138.

Another fact of the false speaking in tongues is that as it is generated from demons, it tends towards looseness in emotions and even towards the sexual emotions. This sad fact is not far wanting in historical proof.

"The doctrines of free love and "spiritual marriages" have too often appeared in association with tongues. Perversion of the biblical teaching relating to sex and marriage can be seen in the Mormons and the Shakers. Aimee Semple Mc Pherson was not the only tongues leader to receive a "revelation" that her marriage was "not in the Lord" and that she should enter another union. One of the serious problems of the Pentecostal movement has been the fact

that many of its leaders have fallen into immorality. One well-known pentecostal preacher, a woman widowed for three years, professed to be "with child of the Holy Ghost"...Bauman quotes one young man as saying, "To my surprise, I found that these blessed emotions in my soul seemed to be accompanied with sexual passion in my body." I have a sad clipping in my Bible telling of how a famous Pentecostal evangelist was found dead in a San Francisco hotel. An autopsy proved he was an alcoholic and was killed by an excess of liquor." **Ibid.**, pp. 149-150.

Not *even* the founder of Pentecostalism in 1901 Charles Fox Parham escaped the immoralities that came from the looseness of emotions fostered by spiritistic "tongues speaking". Observe:

"Parham, "father of the modern Pentecostal movement", was arrested for the grossest of immoralities." **Ibid.**, p. 149.

So many things are wrong with this "tongues speaking" scandal. Take for example:

"In Pentecostal services, often someone speaks in tongues and another gives what is pretended to be a divinely given "interpretation". But a few words may result in a long interpretation, or a long speech in tongues may be interpreted in few words. Prophesies are made that are never fulfilled." **Ibid.**, p. 150.

As A.E. Ruark says:

"They seek to speak in tongues with the expectation that it is by the "baptism of the Holy Spirit." They thereby put themselves at the disposal of a demon spirit which may give the gift of tongues as a manifestation of the false doctrine." Quoted in Alexander Seibel, **The Church Infiltrated**, p. 55.

CHAPTER 4
THE SECRET RAPTURE

What is Evangelicalism today without the secret rapture? Today, we live in a religious eschatological culture which Pentecostalism/Evangelicalism has fostered. Generally, the "rapture" (catching up) of the church is expected as the next event in their prophetic calendar, then will come seven years in which a personal anti-christ (an individual) will be manifested.

For the first 3 ½ years of the seven years, the anti-christ will make a pact with the Jews who would have restored the temple and animal sacrifices in Jerusalem. But for the last 3 ½ years, the anti-christ will turn upon the Jews and begin to kill them, at which time Christ will come again and fight the anti-christ for the Jews. Only 144,000 Jews will remain alive. Then Christ will set up a kingdom for 1000 years in which the Jews will reign over all the Gentile nations. This teaching which has slight variations of points more or less is the present eschatological (end time) teaching of Evangelicals.

Our enquiry here is not to deal with all the aspects of this teaching for it shall take a great treatise of many pages. Instead we shall deal with the "secret rapture" part of this schema, which no doubt, in all its parts, is equally erroneous. We just find it necessary to deal with the concept of a secret coming of Christ which the Bible warned against, but which has been made so wide-spread and popular through Pentecostal preaching that it is today accepted as gospel truth. That such a teaching could exist among Evangelicals when it is so evidently erroneous shows how often traditional doctrines are held without genuine research in the Bible; thus one would really have to wonder where is the Spirit of Truth that Christ promised? Why is He not in the community of the Evangelicals? Christ told us: "Howbeit when he, the Spirit of truth, is come, he will guide you into all truth: for he shall not speak of himself; but whatsoever he shall hear, that shall he speak: and he will shew you things to come." John 16:13. The "secret rapture" doctrine is not truth, thus it was not revealed by the Spirit, but another spirit was responsible for its existence as shall soon be seen.

A teaching so important as the second coming of Jesus Christ, the blessed hope for all the faithful, cannot afford to be perverted in these end times, for it shall give us a wrong conception of the events that are to occur, thus we shall not be able to be faithful watchmen over our souls and that of others, we shall be in danger of being caught unawares so that the end shall come and we shall not be saved. Certainly this is not the experience of a born again Christian.

Now there are many things wrong about the secret rapture doctrine that can clearly expose it to be the falsehood that it is. For example, to believe the secret rapture, is to believe not only that the second coming of Christ is a secret coming (against Christ's explicit warning in Matthew 24), but to also divide this second coming into two parts- the "secret rapture" part and the "visible appearance" part. Also, if Christ is coming for His church, then the secret rapture would mean that He only comes for part of His church and leaves back the rest for seven years and then comes again for them, unless those that remain after the secret rapture are not His church in any way. If this be so, what are they anyway? And if Christ marries His church as His bride, what will He do to those that He returns for during the "visible appearance" part of His second coming? Will He marry them also? Does He intend to have two wives- one, the church, and the other the Jewish kingdom? If the dispensation of Grace is ended, would the saints who live during the seven-year reign of the anti-christ be saved by something else other than Grace? Also, why would God allow the temple to be rebuilt and animal sacrifices to be again reinstituted? Would that not be denial of Christ? Would that not then encourage righteousness by works as approving to God? And would it not also mean that Christ was never meant by God to be the Saviour of the whole world, seeing that Grace has ended with the secret rapture, and those that live during the seven-year reign of the anti-christ are saved through some other means? There are so many things about this teaching which are definitely wrong and which reveal the teaching as originating from the pit of hell.

Not only can the false tongues doctrine and experience be traced among Evangelicals as originating in "spiritual manifestations" taught to be the Holy Spirit's working, but even this "secret rapture" monstrosity.

In this chapter, we shall attempt to first show the historical origins of the doctrine, then we shall show from scripture how it is wrong.

Now where do we start? Let us start with a description of the secret rapture theory as it is expressed among evangelicals.

> "According to their theory the Lord is to come **SECRETLY** for His saints: they are to be caught up (raptured) to meet Him in the air without the world knowing that anything is happening: all who are unprepared are to be left on earth in an unsaved state; then an individual known as the "Antichrist" is to make his appearance, to assume power as a world Dictator, to revive the old Roman Empire as a ten-kingdomed confederacy, and to rule over it, to make a covenant with the Jews to allow them to set up again their temple worship in Jerusalem, and at the end of three-and-a-half years to break the covenant and persecute them. After seven years Christ is to come back with His saints to destroy the Anti-Christ and set up His reign of a thousand years on this earth. All these things are described in as much detail as if they were actually taught in the Bible, and some good men have got the impression that the Bible does actually contain them." Duncan Mc Gougall, **The Rapture of the Saints**, p. 1.

This is the exact teaching of Pentecostalism. This is a new doctrine, new to the Christian world, and it is not even two hundred years old.

"Pretribulationism [the secret rapture occurring before the tribulation] is a recent view which was formulated 125 years ago...(date of this statement: 1956)." George Eldon Ladd, **The Blessed Hope**, p. 58.

"Although the pretribulational rapture position is highly popular and influential, it is of recent origin – not much more than a hundred and fifty years old...As far as church history can determine, that view cannot be traced further back than about 1830." Robert Van Kampen, **The Sign**, pp. 32, 33.

This "rapture" teaching which places the anti-christ in the future denies all the teachings of the whole Christian church from its inception. When the papal anti-christ appeared from around the fourth century, all the true followers of Christ presented the anti-christ as existing contemporaneously with the true church of God. None of them ever looked for a future anti-christ that would exist only after the rapture of the church, then the anti-christ would do his evil for seven years, then Christ would return and set up a millennial kingdom. This objectionable teaching is called "futurism" and came straight from the Roman Catholic church. However, the rapture theory, coming as it did in the 1830's was added to this futurism teaching of the Catholic church and then mixed with "dispensationalism" which too is a child no older than the 1830's.

That all the prophetic visions of Revelation 4 to 19 including the rise and evils of the anti-christ was to happen only after the so-called rapture was proven to be false by a great bible scholar Dr. Henry Grattan Guinness. We are told of this futurism and placing the anti-christ in the late future...

"...Originated with the astute Ribera [a Jesuit] at the close of the sixteenth century, to relieve the Papacy of the terrible stigma cast upon it by Protestant Reformation interpreters. This was accomplished by getting Antichrist wholly into the future, just as the Preterists had attempted to thrust him entirely into the past. This Futurist view was at first confined to the Romanists, but was taken over in the early nineteenth century by the two Maitlands, Burgh, Tyso, Todd, then the Plymouth Brethren, and some Puseyite expositors. They were thus espoused by opposite groups who, though Protestant, held the Reformation to have been an unwarranted schism, and sought to verge as closely as possible on Rome. Guinness championed the historical School of Protestant view, which holds to the progressive fulfilment of prophecy from John's time to the second advent. Then, following the early church, it came into prominence among the Waldenses, Wyclifites and Hussites, and was embraced by all the Reformers of the sixteenth century. It next became a powerful, formidable weapon motivating the Reformers of Germany, Switzerland, Britain, France, Denmark, and Sweden, and nerving the martyrs of Spain and Italy. It was also held by the earlier Joachim and Brute; as well as by Luther, Zwingli, Melanchthon, Knox, and scores of associates. It was the view of such post – Reformation leaders as Bullinger,

Bale, Foxe, Brightman, Mede, the Pilgrim fathers and Puritan theologians, Sir Isaac and Bishop Newton, Daubuz, Whitson, Faber, Cuninghame, Freve, Birks, Bickersteth, and Elliott – who all agreed on the grand outline ... But both Futurists and Preterists deny the fulfilments recognized by the great mass of solid prophetic interpreters. They have forsaken the main well-trodden highway of interpretation,...for questionable historical evidence and empty speculations about a short-live infidel antichrist to be seated in a literal temple in Palestine. And this character, in the brief compass of 3 ½ years, is to fulfil all the wonders of the Apocalyptic drama, they say, and to exhaust the majestic sweep of prophecy – which the church of God had been blindly misinterpreting and misapplying through the centuries, according to such special methods to do interpretation." Leroy Edwin Froom, **The Prophetic Faith of our Fathers**, Vol. 4. pp. 1196-1197.

Now, let us go directly into historical circumstances that led to the development and spread of the Rapture. Who started the Rapture teaching? We are told by some historians that it was a man by the name of Edward Irving. Who is Edward Irving? He was a Scottish Presbyterian minister who was born in west Scotland in 1792 and died in 1834. In the church which he pastored we are told of the amazing things that happened.

"Then the "unknown tongues" were first manifested in his congregation in October, 1831. The discourse was interrupted by an outbreak of the "utterances." Controversy developed over the origin

of the phenomenon – whether of divine or demonic possession. The attempted prosecution for heresy in December, 1830, had led to Irving's withdrawal from the jurisdiction of the London Presbyter. But he was soon removed from his pulpit by the church trustees, in 1832. The larger part of the congregation-about 800- adhered to him and were forced to seek temporary quarters. They then formed the "Holy Catholic Apostolic Church," popularly known as the Irvingite church." Leroy Edwin Froom, **The Prophetic Faith of our Fathers**, Vol. 3, pp. 516-517.

The so-called gift of "tongues" first appeared in 1831 in Mr. Irving's church, but it was not the real tongues speaking as in the Bible (which we have dealt with in two previous chapters), it was the manifestation of satanic tongues speaking which would later appear in 1901. It was this man that first preached the rapture.

"...there (are) as equal number of scholars who give Edward Irving (considered the father of modern-day Pentecostalism) credit for discovering the dual parousia or coming of Christ, and he has been the most logical candidate until recent years. William Kimball, in his book **The Rapture, A Question of Timing**...*makes this interesting observation: "However, the concept of a pretribulation rapture did not seem to surface in Irving's teachings until the early 1830's, even though the futuristic groundwork has been carefully prepared at the Albury Conferences. However, it has been clearly authenticated that Irving was one of the first to suggest this theory. He is frequently accredited with being a major accomplice in the*

birth of pretribulational teaching." Robert Van Kampen, **The Sign**, pp. 445-446.

"Pretribulationalism arose in the mid-nineteenth century. The likelihood is that Edward Irving was the first to suggest the pretribulation rapture, or at least the seminal thought behind it." Robert Gundry, **The Church and the Tribulation**, p. 185.

"...and Irving is commonly supposed to have been the first [to] mention in the whole history of the church of a SECRET rapture of the saints prior to Christ's appearing in glory." Duncan Mc Dougall, **The Rapture of the Saints**, p. 21.

But where did Mr. Irving get that teaching from? Not from the Bible. Observe:

"And at this very time Irving heard what he believed to be a voice from heaven commanding him to preach the Secret Rapture of the Saints. Obeying this voice, he began to preach that Christ was to come TWICE; first secretly FOR His saints: then, after an interval of seven years – the reign of Antichrist – gloriously with His saints, to destroy Antichrist and to reign." **Ibid.**, p. 21.

Let us look a little longer and deeper at this "voice" that told Mr. Irving to preach a secret rapture. What do we find?

*"Irvingism set forth a sort of Futurism, and a pretribulation "rapture". In **The Morning Watch** Irving explains that although*

> he has not abandoned his former "symbolical" Historicist interpretation of the trumpets, he now expects, on the basis of the revelations of "the Holy Ghost," "by other tongues," a future "literal" fulfilment of these prophecies in England." Leroy Edwin Froom, **The Prophetic Faith of our Fathers**, Vol. 4, p. 1222.

Thus we discover that Mr. Irving was depending upon manifestations of "The Holy Ghost", "by other tongues," or the speaking in tongues deception, as we now know, to get his prophetic doctrines. Here is further proof:

> "I am not aware that there was any definite teaching that there would be a secret rapture of the church at a secret coming until this was given forth as an utterance in Mr. Irving's church, from what was there being received as being the Voice of a Spirit. But whether anyone ever asserted such a thing or not, it was from that supposed revelation that the modern doctrine and the modern phraseology arose. It came not from Holy Scripture, but from that which falsely pretended to be the Spirit of God." Dr. Samuel. P. Tregelles, **The Hope of Christ's Second Coming**, p. 35.

This Dr. Tregelles, a great New Testament scholar was a contemporary of Mr. Irving and knew of the strange happenings at Mr. Irving's church. This leads us to search for who was speaking in tongues and uttering prophecies in Mr. Irving's church, from where he derived his "secret rapture" doctrine and thus began to preach it. We do not have to search very far, for the information is readily available. We come to the Mc Donald family, to the youngest sister yet in her teens at the time she was a member of Mr. Irving's church. Her name is Margaret Mc Donald. Of her it is said:

> *"Margaret Mc Donald was also a semi-invalid. Early in 1830 she had an experience in which she received, she said, "the gift of prophecy." And a little later...the two Mc Donald brothers had a similar experience and each "spoke in tongues."* Arnold Dallimore,
> **Forerunner of the Charismatic Movement**, p.122.

It was from this unstable and deluded teenaged girl that Mr. Irving received this "voice" revealing and telling him to preach the "secret rapture". This was the first time in history such a teaching ever surfaced in Christianity.

> *"...the new understanding of the rapture was the product of a prophetic vision given to a young Scottish girl, Margaret Mac Donald in 1830. She claimed special insight into the second coming and began to share her views with others. Her ecstatic conduct and apocalyptic teaching led to a charismatic renewal in Scotland."*
> Walter A. Elwell, editor, **Evangelical Dictionary of Theology**, pp. 908-909.

It is important to note, that though many Evangelicals claim that the Bible is the source of the secret rapture teaching, in fact, it did not come from the Bible, nor was Miss Mc Donald's visions tested by the

Bible. It was simply believed by a fearful, vacillating and credulous Mr. Irving, who presented it to the public as Bible truth.

> *"Irving was himself teaching a form of the "rapture" which he derived from the "utterances" of the unknown tongues, sometime between 1830 and 1832."* Leroy Edwin Froom, **The Prophetic Faith of our Fathers**, Vol. 4, p. 1224.

But by far the more authoritative evidence for Miss Margaret Mc Donald as the original source of the secret rapture teaching comes from a medical doctor Mr. Robert Norton, who recorded the event in a book that he wrote in 1861. The statement reads as follows:

> *"Marvelous light was shed upon scripture, and especially on the doctrine of the second Advent, by the revived spirit of prophecy. In the following account by Miss M. M. [Margaret Mac Donald], of an evening during which the power of the Holy Ghost rested upon her for several successive hours, in mingling prophecy and vision, we have an instance; for here we first see the distinction between the final stage of the Lord's coming, when every eye shall see Him [the second parousia], and His prior appearing in glory to them that look for Him [the first parousia]."* Robert Norton, **The Restoration of Apostles and Prophets in the Catholic Apostolic Church**. Quoted from Robert Van Kampen, **The Sign**, p. 446.

This and this only, is the origin of the "secret rapture" or two part second coming of Christ so espoused by Evangelicals today; it came not from the Bible, but from the excited mind of an unstable teenaged girl who had her "speaking in tongues" interpreted, and out of it came this secret rapture heresy. In the year 1833 a meeting was organized by a Lady Powerscourt at her castle in London. To it came Edward Irving and others, including a man that would later be the leader of the Brethren group and founder of what is called "Dispensationalism", this man is John Nelson Darby.

Mr. Darby presented his "dispensation" teachings which did not yet include the Rapture and the seven year antichrist reign, but he heard such a theory for the first time from Irving who presented it at the Powerscourt Conference. That the rapture theory first made the light of day in the Powerscourt Conferences had been recorded.

> "It was in these meetings that the precious truth of the rapture of the church was brought to light; that is, the coming of the Lord in the air to take away His church before the great tribulation should begin on earth. The views of Brethren elsewhere, but as years went on obtained wide publication in denominational circles, chiefly through the writings of such men as Darby, Bellet, Newton, S.P. Tregelles, Andrew Jukes, Wigram, and after 1845 William Kelly, whose name was then linked with the movement; C. H. Mackintosh, Charles Stanley, J. B. Stoney and others." Harry

Ironside, **A Historical Sketch of the Brethren Movement**, p. 23.

At the Powerscourt meetings Irving and his party rejected Darby's Dispensationalism and pulled out of the meetings. Apparently, Darby got to know that Mr. Irving got his rapture teaching by "utterances" and "tongues" from Margaret Mc Donald, and he visited her. We are told:

> "According to his own testimony in later years he met Margaret Mac Donald, but rejected her claims of a new outpouring of the Spirit. Despite his opposition to Mac Donald's general approach some writers believe that he accepted her view of the rapture and worked it into his own system." Walter A. Elwell, editor, **Evangelical Dictionary of Theology**, p. 909.

Then it was Mr. John Darby that spread this rapture theory with the seven year antichrist reign mixed into his dispensational teaching. What can we conclude about Mr. Edward Irving? Of him it is said:

> "But he was somewhat lacking in mental poise. His leaning to mysticism, which provoked the apprehension of Chalmers, left him ill – guarded against religious eccentricity. He gave too ready an ear to those who were ambitious to unfold the mysteries of prophecy, and was led to over value the miracle as a means of advancing Christianity. Accordingly, when a strange spirit of prophesying broke out in his congregation (1831), he encouraged it, under the supposition that the gift of tongues had been renewed... The babel

of strange voices at the Caledonian church was a source of derision to some and of grief to others. The matter tended seriously to compromise the position of Irving." Henry C. Sheldon, **History of the Christian Church**, Vol. 5, pp. 195-196.

And what happened to Mr. Irving's Catholic Apostolic Church, even after he died a broke man in 1834? It is said:

"As in the case of Dr. Maitland and the Tractarians, so in the case of Irving. His obedience to the "voice" which commanded him to preach the Secret Rapture seems to have been the signal for loosing of a veritable deluge of "spirit manifestations" upon him and his poor deluded congregation. The result was a fanatical outbreak which scandalized the whole church. Led by a Mr. Robert Baxter, who is described as "for a time one of the most deluded men in the church's History," who gave utterance to the most extraordinary prophecies and angel communications, which were accepted as truths by the infatuated people, the congregation went from one fanatical extreme to another, till what had been a Presbyterian congregation formally applied for admission to the Church of Rome." Duncan Mc Dougall, **The Rapture of the Saints**, pp. 23-24.

And this is just where the Evangelical churches are going, indeed many of them have already signed accords of working together with the Roman Church as seen in the notorious **Evangelicals and Catholics**

Together document; the Charismatic Movement has caused a bond of sympathy and acceptance between the two movements.

However, let's hear what Mr. Baxter of the Irvingite Church admitted when he repented.

> *"Mr. Robert Baxter subsequently repented deeply of his part in the impiety. Humbly confessing his sin, he separated himself wholly from the partisans of the "fables" and published a "Narrative of the Facts". He constantly maintained that the manifestations with which he had been connected were supernatural, but that Satan, not the Holy Spirit, was their author. This explains the features of the movement. It is notable that the whole movement including the origin of the "secret rapture" idea, belongs to the era when the three unclean and delusive spirits like frogs began to go forth. It would therefore be part of their work."* **The Rapture of the Saints**, p. 24.

At this time Mr. Evangelical, we say to you: How can you claim the secret rapture to be a Biblical teaching after all the evidences that has been shown to you? Can you not see that it is time to drop it out of your system of beliefs like some Evangelicals have wisely done? It is not Biblical teaching at all as Mr. Mc Dougall has shown.

> *"There is not a Bible teacher nor anyone else living in the world today who has found a secret rapture in the Bible by his own independent study of the Bible itself. These teachers all come to the*

Bible with cut-and-dried theories which they have learnt elsewhere, and twist and torture text to fit the theory." **Ibid.**, pp. 45-46.

Now in returning to the man who first spread the secret rapture theory mixed with his dispensational speculations – John Nelson Darby, we find that not only did he convert the Brethren Movement of that teaching, but it was him that first spread it to America.

> *"It was the contribution of John Nelson Darby to eschatology that led many Christians to teach that the return of Christ would be in two stages: one for his saints at the rapture and the other with his saints to control the world at the close of the great tribulation...Darby's ideas had a wide influence in Britain and the United States. Many Evangelicals became pretribulationists through the preaching of the interdenominal evangelists of the nineteenth and twentieth centuries."* Walter A. Elwell, **Evangelical Dictionary of Theology**, p. 908.

> *"Darby visited America six times between 1859 and 1874 and was warmly welcomed. His system of prophetic interpretation was eagerly adopted..."* George Eldon Ladd, **The Blessed Hope**, p. 43.

Then there are the Niagara Conferences where Darby's system was accepted by many ministers, though some of them later denied the rapture teaching.

"Another series of meetings of even greater importance was that which met at Niagara on Lake Ontario from 1883-1897. This conference was the outgrowth of a small Bible study fellowship initiated in 1875 by a handful of men among whom were Nathaniel West, J. H. Brookes and W. J. Erdman. They were joined the next year by A. J. Gordon. This group met from place to place until the conference at Ontario was undertaken. Among the leading teachers of the Ontario conferences, according to A. C. Gaebelein, were James H. Brooks, A. J. Gordon, W. J. Erdman, Albert Erdman, George C. Needham, A. C. Dickson, I. W. Mundhall, H M. Parsons, Canon Howitt, E. P. G. Moorehead and A. T. Pierson. After this pioneer of American Bible conferences was discontinued, a new conference at Seacliff, Long Island, was opened in 1901, and it was here that the plan for the Reference Bible embodying the dispensational system of interpretation occurred to Dr. C. I. Scofield ... Many of the teachers at the Niagara Conference accepted J. N. Darby's pretribulation rapture along with the doctrine of Christ's return. Of the men named above, James H. Brookes, A. T. Pierson, and C. I. Scofield have been among the most influential supporters of this view." **Ibid.**, pp. 44-45.

Also Cyrus I. Scofield edited a reference Bible that contained J. N. Darby's dispensationalism with the rapture theory as a part of it. This Bible with its brief notes became the Bible of the blossoming Evangelical Movement in the early 1900s, and through it the rapture and kindred heresies spread.

*"The **Scofield Reference Bible** and the leading Bible institutes and graduate schools of theology such as Dallas Theological Seminary, Talbot Seminary, and Grace Theological Seminary also contributed to the popularity of this view."* Walter A. Elwell, editor, **Evangelical Dictionary of Theology**, p. 908.

We have finally arrived at the end of how a theory given to a teenaged, excitable, demon possessed girl, having no Biblical scholarship or learning whatsoever was able to transverse time and become the actual belief of millions of Evangelicals all over the earth. However, wherever it is believed, it is never through the fruit of genuine spirit directed Bible study, because this cannot confirm the rapture of Margaret Mc Donald or even the dispensationalism of Mr. J. N. Darby. There are many great Evangelical Bible scholars who, after having once dogmatically believed the rapture theory, have researched the Bible and given it up totally.

There are so many of them that if we were to give their story, it would make this chapter extremely long beyond the intention of the writer. However we can give an example of some of the writers' comments as they gave up the theory of the rapture as a falsehood.

A. J. Gordon, famed pastor of Clarendon Street Baptist Church in Boston, in his book Ecce Venit, 1889 gave up Darby's system saying: "Where a judaizing interpretation would lead us from this phrase of the apostle, to imagine a future temple rebuild in Jerusalem, enthroning an infidel anti-Christ..." Dr. W. J. Erdman in renouncing the rapture in his tract A Theory Revived said: "Better the disappointment of truth than the fair but false promises of error." Robert Cameron gave up the rapture also. In his book of 1922 – **Scriptural Truth About The Lord's Return**, he said this extremely true and penetrating statement: "Everywhere in the New Testament it is taught that to suffer for Christ is one of the highest honors Christians can have bestowed upon them. A desire to shirk suffering for Christ is a sign of degeneracy." Henry W. Frost in 1924 wrote Matthew Twenty-Four and The Revelation, in which he gave up the rapture. He said: "This view might be held as truth if there were any scripture to confirm it, but [it] may not be held in view of the fact that no scripture even suggest such a process of events and many scriptures positively contradict it ..." W. G. Moorehead of Xenia Theological Seminary from 1873 to 1914 was also a consulting editor of the Scofield Reference Bible. Of him we are also told:

> *"Here is a clear rejection by an editor of the Scofield Bible of the pretribulation rapture of the Church with the two comings of Christ which is found in the Scofield Bible."* George Eldon Ladd, **The Blessed Hope**, p. 50.

Charles R. Erdman in his book **The Return of Christ** also rejected the rapture, though he contributed to the formation of the Scofield Reference Bible. He said: "The doctrine appears to be founded upon a false interpretation of the translation, in the King James Version ..." James H. Brookes in his book **Maranatha** renounces the theory saying: "The Darby view of a pre-tribulation rapture was accepted without much question or careful study." Philip Mauro, a lawyer, in his book **The Gospel of the Kingdom** (1928) renounced the rapture and also dispensationalism. He said: "... the Scofield Bible has usurped the place of authority that belongs to God's Bible alone." Dr. Harold John Ockenga, Pastor of Park Street Church, Boston in **Christian Life** (February 1955) showed his rejection of the rapture theory. What he said is very interesting: "It is conceivable that the Jews without the Pentecostal presence and power of the Holy Spirit will do in the tribulation what the church in the Holy Spirit power could not in 2,000 years? No amount of explaining can make (1 Thessalonians 4:16,17) a secret rapture. It is the visible accompaniment of the glorious advent of the Lord." These were just some of the many scholars that gave up the rapture theory. In a summary of this evidence which were all taken from Mr. Ladd's **The Blessed Hope**, we can quote him again saying:

> "...many devout men who first accepted this teaching were later, upon mature study, compelled to reverse themselves and admit that they could not find this doctrine in the Word of God." **Ibid.,** p. 61.

Will you too Mr. Evangelical give up this false teaching? Will you now bow your head in prayer and ask God to give you courage to reject this teaching and follow on to know the Truth and where ever it shall take you? Get down now on your knees in prayer for a while, and then take your Bible and read over the scriptures that have been used to prove a secret rapture. Now you would see that there is nothing secret about it, that those scriptures do not support a double second coming of Jesus Christ. After this great exposure, you cannot believe that error and still hope to be saved. It is impossible for you to ignore the voice of the Spirit talking to you and still call yourself a born-again Christian.

Now let us finally look at the two major scriptures that Evangelicals use to prove the "secret rapture", and then we shall look at a few more. These scriptures are Matthew 24:37-41 and 1 Thessalonians 4:15-17. Let us first deal with Matthew 24:37-41 which says: *"But as the days of Noe were, so shall also the coming of the Son of man be. For as in the days that were before the flood they were eating and drinking, marrying and giving in marriage, until the day that Noe entered into the ark, And knew not until the flood came, and took them all away; so shall also the coming of the Son of man be. Then shall two be in the field; the one shall be taken, and the other left. Two women shall be grinding at the mill; the one shall be taken, and the other left. Watch therefore: for ye know not what hour your Lord doth come."* This text speaks about one second coming. By telling us *"... as the days of Noe were so shall also the coming of the Son of man be."* (verse 37). The "coming" referred to in that verse is not an isolated account of the coming first introduced in the verse. Other different accounts of that SAME second coming are referred to in the same chapter, and none of them even hints at a "secret" coming, or even the continuing of civilization after that coming. Let us look at some verses in the chapter that confirm what was just said.

In the first instance, Christ is answering questions concerning His second coming asked by certain disciples.

Observe: *"And as he sat on the Mount of Olives, the disciples came unto him privately, saying, Tell us, when shall these things be? And what shall be the sign of thy coming, and of the end of the world?"* Matthew 24:3. Here we see the second coming of Christ is equated with *"... the end of the world ..."* not its continuation under the antichrist. Thus Christ's answers must show the end of society at His second coming not its continuation. There is nothing secret about this coming. As Christ gives His discourse upon things that will happen before He comes He speaks about, *"... wars and rumours of wars..."* and says *"... but the end is not yet."* (verse. 6). This shows that He is coming to show the **end**, not a partial end or anything of the sort, but the end of the world, this is what His coming refers to. In verse 13 He says: "But he that shall endure unto the end, the same shall be saved."

This reveals a great persecution that is to come upon the church just before He comes, and the church must endure, thus there is no catching up before the tribulation, the church must go through the tribulation as many other scriptures show (e.g. John 16:1-3,33; 2 Timothy 3:12; Revelation 6:7-11; Revelation 12:11,13-17; Revelation **13:11**-17; Revelation 7:13-17). In Matthew 24:21,22 a great tribulation is referred to, but nothing is said of the church being raptured before it, in fact, it is the church that faces this tribulation. Verses 23-26 gives a warning about false prophets that show signs and wonders to convince many of a coming Christ that the whole world does not see. This, in a sense, attacks any form of secret coming like the "secret rapture", and Jesus then shows the real nature of the ONE second coming. He says: "...For as the lightning cometh out of the east, and shineth even unto the west; so shall also the coming of the son of man be. For wheresoever the carcase is, there will the eagles be gathered together." Matthew 24:27,28.

Obviously, the example Christ gives against any form of secret coming is that everyone on the earth will see. Lightning striking at one end of the sky will be seen at the other end. When the eagles are seen in mass circling an area in the sky (and they can be seen from afar), then one knows that a carcase is in the area on the ground below; so where Jesus is when He comes in the air, the righteous will be seen gathered together unto Him. This knocks down any notion of a secret coming and the continuation of society. In Matthew 24:30,31 Christ continues to explain this one second coming: *'And then shall appear the sign of the Son of man in heaven: and then shall all the tribes of the earth mourn, and they shall see the Son of man coming in the clouds of heaven with power and great [Gk.vast] glory. And he shall send his angels with a great sound of a trumpet, and they shall gather together his elect from the four winds, from one end of heaven to the other."*

What can be plainer than this? Here we are told that *"all the tribes of the earth"* shall mourn, and *'they shall see the Son of man coming'*; this is the same **one** second coming, and everyone shall **see** it. What is so secret about that? Nothing, nothing at all! When Christ is coming, He shall be seen with "vast" (according to the Greek text) glory. Why is this so? Because a little lower down in Matthew 25:31, Christ explained that "When the Son of man shall come in his glory, and all the holy angels with him, ...", and in Matthew 16:27 He also said: *"For the Son of man shall come in the glory of his Father with his angels; ..."* Think about this. This **one** second coming of Christ will see a "vast" display of the glory of the Father, the glory of Christ and obviously the glory of all the holy angels, since they accompany Christ. No wonder why *"that wicked"* (the antichrist) shall be *destroyed "... with the brightness of his coming."* 2 Thessalonians 2:8. How plain can we become? Can you not see Mr. Evangelical that there is not any secret rapture but the visible appearance of Christ at which the world shall be destroyed?

You must read the following texts which speak about the same event. They are Isaiah 2:12-21; Isaiah 13:9-13; Isaiah 24:1-6,17-23; Isaiah 26:21; Isaiah 34:1-8.

Now let us return to Matthew 24. Verses 32-34 show us how we can know when Christ's coming is near. Verse 36 tells us that only the Father knows when the second coming will be. Then we come to verses 37-42, the block of scriptures which Evangelicals like to quote to support their secret rapture theory, but which evidently does not, as it is referring to the **one** second coming referred to in the other verses above.

But what is this block of scripture telling us? A careful reading will reveal that the comment given by Jesus in verse 42 is the real point. It says: *"Watch therefore: for ye know not what hour your Lord doth come."* This is obviously not a physical looking up into the sky to see when Christ would come; it is a spiritual watch over one's moral state. We are to be abiding in Christ so as not to become like the *"evil servant"* (Read

Matthew 24:45-51). The deeds of the evil servant show that he was a backslider yet professing to be a true Christian like the lukewarm people of Revelation 3:14-17. In fact lukewarmness was his real state because he did not watch care over his moral state according to the admonitions in Revelation 3:18-22. When Christ therefore comes for the righteous to take them with Him, the evil servant is left behind *"...in the field..."* or *"... at the mill ..."* (Matthew 24:40,41), and according to Matthew 24:51 is *"cut ...asunder..."* There is no seven-year anti-christ reign after that, but all the remaining wicked are destroyed at the **one** second coming of Christ. There is no second chance for anyone; either you are ready at His second coming, or you are not, because you did not watch care over your moral state.

There is no secret rapture here. None at all! How was it in Noah's day according to Matthew 24:37-39? The wicked were in the worship of their false gods, they were in feasting, riotings, revelry and all sorts of corruption until the flood came and took them all away. So will be the wicked today, until the coming of Christ will take them all away into destruction. The parable of two in the field and at the mill with one taken and the other left is merely to show us that while people will be in the pursuit of their daily chores, one would have been ready and one would not be ready. This is why one was taken and the other left back into utter destruction. Those left back when Noah and his family were taken in the ark did not live on for a few more years and have another chance to be saved by their own martyrdom (oh, this is so silly); no, they were immediately destroyed by the flood that followed; so also will those that are left back at the second coming of Christ, they will all be slaughtered by the brightness of His second coming. Thus the text in no way shows some "secret" coming or rapture of the saints, it is folly to claim this. Christ's Olivet discourse continues in the whole of Matthew 25, and nowhere do we see a secret rapture with those remaining behind having a second chance during some seven-year anti-christ reign.

All the parables of Matthew 25 are to admonish people how to be prepared for that one second coming of Christ; you see, because there is no second chance; when He comes everyone will be either saved or lost and that's it.

The parable of the wise and foolish virgins in Matthew 25:1-13 ends with the wicked being lost at the one second coming of Christ. In verse 12 Christ tells them *"... I know you not."* Then comes the comment warning us to watch our moral state.

The next parable that follows in Matthew 25:14-30 is of the same kind as the preceding one and at the second coming of Christ there is no second chance for the wicked on the basis of their relationship to the anti-christ. Those who are morally irresponsible at the second coming of Christ are destroyed. It is recorded as being *"... cast...into outer darkness."* (Verse 30). Then comes the final parable in the last block of scriptures which covers Matthew 25:31-46. It starts with the visible coming of Christ with the holy angels as we were told before, and ends with no second chance for the wicked. We are told that they shall "...go away into everlasting punishment." (Verse 46). And this brings us to the end of Christ's Olivet's discourse.

In it, we can fully summarize, there is not even the slightest hint at anything called a "secret rapture" as told to us by Evangelicals, because it is not in the Bible, but it simply came from demons who interfered with a silly, teenaged, excited girl who interpreted her false tongues utterances to mean a rapture. We can now come to the next major scripture used by Evangelicals to support a secret rapture, namely 1 Thessalonians 4:15-17. It says: *"For this we say unto you by the word of the Lord, that we which are alive and remain [Gk. Survive] unto the coming of the Lord shall not prevent [Gk. Precede] them which are asleep. For the Lord himself shall descend from heaven with a shout, with the voice of the archangel, and with the trump of God: and the dead in Christ shall rise first: Then we which are alive and remain [Gk. Survive] shall be caught up together with them in the clouds, to meet the Lord in the air: and so shall we ever be with the Lord."* This text is used to prove the secret rapture. How can Evangelicals do such a thing is beyond me. Nothing in the text even implies a secret coming of Christ. In fact, it shows that when Christ comes the world will know by the noise that is being made.

In **verse 16** we have the noise of a *"shout"* (but the Greek says summons), when the voice of the archangel calls awake the sleeping hosts of righteousness. We have also the trump of God which is the sound of a great trumpet that is heard and is recorded in Matthew 24:31. Now, with all those noises and the great heat from all that glory and the shaking of the earth, how can this be a secret coming? Of Jesus who spoke on Mt. Sinai to the children of Israel it is said: "Whose voice then shook the earth :but now he had promised, saying, Yet once more I shake not the earth only, but also the heaven" Hebrews 12:26. Thus the voice of the archangel (Jesus-Daniel 10:5-9,21; Daniel 12:1; Jude 9), will shake the heavens as it is *"... departed as a scroll when it is rolled together ..."* Revelation 6:14-17; this is not a secret coming of Christ. 1 Thessalonians 4:15-17 in no way speaks of a secret rapture. Furthermore verse 15 tells us that the living saints will be those which "remain", or "survive" according to the Greek text. Survive what? The great persecution that is to come upon the last church as is referred to in Revelation 6:11, thus the church is to be caught up only after it has faced the final persecution, not before, read Revelation 12:17. Here we do not see the slightest reference to the "secret rapture" ideas propagated by Evangelicals. Finally, neither does 1 Corinthians 15:51,52 show a secret rapture.

The word "mystery" referred to by Paul in verse 51 does not mean "secret" but an unknown thing that is revealed, this is why he said *"Behold I **shew** you a mystery..."* and, furthermore, he is speaking about the change from earthly flesh to a new heavenly flesh at the second coming, but he is not especially speaking about the second coming.

However, he refers to the same "trump" in verse 52 that he spoke of in 1 Thessalonians 4:16, and which Christ referred to in Matthew 24:31. This noise certainly does not refer to a secret coming and hence shows the rapture to be what it is, a human invention, or, if you prefer to call it doctrines of devils

CHAPTER 5

THE "SPECULATIVE NONSENSE" OF DARBY'S DISPENSATIONALISM

The heading of this chapter is not meant to be a ridicule, in fact, it is not the words of the author that Dispensationalism is called "speculative nonsense", though the term is a most perfect one. This phrase was used by one, Newton, who criticized Darby's dispensational teachings.

> "Darby was keen on a belief of his own, which the Brethren lovingly refer to as "Dispensational Truth," but which Newton called "speculative nonsense." Duncan Mc Dougall, **The Rapture of the Saints**, p. 43.

Most Evangelicals used the word "Dispensation" in an effort to show that the Law of God and the Sabbath are no longer relevant for man to keep, but they have never understood what "dispensations" are all about, neither have they been able to define them and prove them from the Bible. Yet it has been convenient for them to use the word to reject obedience to God's law especially where the Sabbath is concerned. Because they have used the word "Dispensation" it has now become necessary for us to explain a little about it, because this is another false teaching which will damn anyone who believes in it and render them not "born again" Christians.

In Mr. Wordsworth N. Caesar's attacks upon the Law of God, the Sabbath and diet reform, he constantly uses the phrase "Dispensation of Grace" over and over, so at this time we shall quote extensively from one of his books to show how he uses the term as an Evangelical.

> *"Therefore, as far as the Church of Jesus Christ is concerned, there remains no obligation whatsoever for a christian to subscribe to any of the aforementioned ordinances, in this dispensation of Grace. I repeat, no true christian has anything to gain by the espousal of any commandment relating to NEW MOON observance, discrimination against UNCLEAN MEATS, being or not being CIRCUMCISED in the flesh, or the observance of any SABBATH day or days, in this dispensation of grace."* Wordsworth N. Caesar, **The Middle Wall of Partition that Jesus Christ Broke Down**, p. vii.

What do we get from that statement? That certain ordinances, commandments, new moon observances, circumcision, the seventh-day sabbath and other sabbaths all belonged to another past dispensation, but are not relevant to this dispensation of grace. While the things identified in his statement are a "hodge-podge" of confusion and misrepresentations, it is the use of dispensations we are interested in.

"Now although they were appropriate for the Jews under the first covenant, and shall then be obligatory for Jews and Gentiles in the Millennium, they are certainly contrary to the nature of the christian in THIS DISPENSATION of grace." **Ibid.**, p. vii (Emphasis original).

This tells me that keeping the law and the sabbath, and also vegetarianism was relevant for Jews under the old covenant which was in a past dispensation, but now under the new dispensation of grace, they are wrong and would render us not Christians if we do them. Of course, this would mean that so long as God has these things existing under the old covenant and past dispensation, nobody could ever be a Christian. Thus by extension two types of people will be saved, they are Jews under the past dispensation, and Christians under a different dispensation.

Further it is really the height of "speculative nonsense" for God to make both Jews and Gentiles keep what is called the old covenant because they are in the millennium (which is another dispensation).

"For whereas the meeting place of God and man under the old covenant was the ark of the covenant - Ex. 25:22 - the meeting place in this dispensation of grace, is now the individual spirits of each member of the Body of Christ." **Ibid.**, p. 11.

A statement like this makes us think or deduce that God did not meet in man's individual spirit in the old dispensation as He now does

69

in the dispensation of Grace. Then how in heaven's name has He really communicated to the average Israelite who had no access to the ark of the covenant or to any priest? We would have to conclude that they were doomed to remain godless.

> "This being so, brethren, it is indeed religious folly for anyone to desire to be a GRAFTED-IN-JEW, whatever that means. For there is no advantage whatsoever in being Jewish in this dispensation, once one is a true member of the Body of Christ (the church)." **Ibid.**, p. 16.

If this be the case, we would have to ask God why He made it an advantage to be a Jew (not favouring us Gentiles) under the old dispensation? This teaching is so much "speculative nonsense".

> "In this new dispensation of grace, those Jewish laws have no place." **Ibid.**, pg. 4.

Then why God did not give grace from the beginning? Why has He not divided up man by dispensations? If grace could save now, then it ought to have been able to save men before.

> "The liberty to eat any type of meat in this dispensation is put beyond question, when one considers 1 Timothy 4:1-4, which states emphatically that all doctrines that put restrictions on the believer, with respect to the forbidding of meats in this dispensation of grace must be satanically inspired." **Ibid.**, p. 49.

Well then, we can eat elephant meat, lion meat, dog meat, carrion crow meat, snake meat or even roaches, ants and worms, since they are all composed of meat. We can sacrifice our health now in this dispensation of grace, while the former dispensation protected the Jews only.

Friends, is this the kind of God you want to serve? Is not this idea of dispensation much "speculative nonsense"? Now as to where a dispensation begins or ends, and the amount of dispensations there are, is left up to the particular sect in Evangelicalism to which one belongs. However, there are basically seven dispensations that are usually agreed to. Here is a fair enough representation of this teaching from Mr. Clarence Larkin in his book **Dispensational Truth or God's Plan and Purpose in the Ages**. He tells us:

> *"This Dispensation [the first] extends from the creation of Adam to the Expulsion from the garden. As to its duration we know nothing. It was probably very short and was the "Dispensation of Innocence."* **Ibid.**, p. 32.

I can add that we know not how the moral state of Adam and Eve, before sin, can be called a Dispensation. This is not a Biblical teaching.

Now about the second dispensation we are told:

> *"This Dispensation extends from the "Fall" to the "Flood". It lasted for 1656 years and was the Dispensation of "Conscience". It shows what man will do when guided only by his conscience. Adam*

71

ARE EVANGELICALS TRUE BORN AGAIN CHRISTIANS?

and Eve had no conscience before the "Fall". Conscience is a knowledge of good and evil, and this Adam and Eve did not have until they ate of the fruit of the forbidden tree. Conscience may produce fear and remorse, but it will not keep men from doing wrong, for conscience imparts no "power". **Ibid.**, p. 34.

There are so many things wrong with this Dispensation and the things said in it. For example, if God knows that conscience imparts no power to keep men from sin, why did He not give Grace or something to help man? Why doom man to 1656 years of failure, "fear" and "remorse"?

Also, if transgression gave Adam and Eve a knowledge of good and evil which is conscience, then transgression gave them a good thing which gives them fear and remorse in transgression. What can we say about this? It is so much "speculative nonsense".

Here is the third Dispensation.

"This was the Dispensation of "Human Government". If ever the human race had an opportunity to work out the theory of "Human Government" it was right after the flood." **Ibid.**, p.37.

What is he saying? If today we are saved by Grace in the dispensation of Grace, then what was man saved by in this third dispensation? Was it by human government? Or was God just allowing men to experiment with government? What does that have to do with salvation? Besides, there has been no time that men have been allowed

72

to experiment with government until since 1776 A.C.B., after the American independence, up to today.

Before this, all governments were Monarchies, but now we have had Republicanism, Communism, Parliamentary Democracy, Monarchy, Fascism etc. So now is the time the theory has really been stretched to its limits and not in the time of the third Dispensation. All this makes this Dispensation of human government fall flat as mere "speculative nonsense". Now for the fourth Dispensation.

"This dispensation extended from the "Call of Abraham" to the "Exodus", a period of 430 years, and is known as the Dispensation of "The Family" **Ibid.**, p. 38.

What is this all about? Are we saved by the family as contrasted to Grace in the Dispensation of Grace? What sense do we make of this? Is it that God dealt only with families at that time? Does He not deal with families now as He has always done? One becomes lost at the sense portrayed in this folly. Is this real? Do we not see that all this Dispensation talk is as Mr. Norton really said? So much "speculative nonsense." Here now is the fifth dispensation.

"This Dispensation extended from the "Exodus" to the "Birth of Christ", a period of 1491 (?) years, and is known as the dispensation of the "law". **Ibid.**, p. 38.

This is the Dispensation Mr. Caesar referred to as past when the various laws and diets of Israel were beneficial to Jews. You see, some

Evangelicals love to use the phrases "Dispensation of Law", and "Dispensation of Grace" to confine obedience to the law and Sabbath-keeping to the past or to an era where they would not have to see the need for keeping them. But the doing of this is an evil impulse, because who would justifiably want to depreciate obedience to God's law and at the same time expect to be saved? This is not Bible religion.

Additionally, what does the Dispensation of "law" mean? Does it mean that people were saved by law in that dispensation and not by grace? Does God therefore have two ways of saving men? Or does He have two wives, one Israel and the other the church? Or, to put it morally clear- is God a polygamist? All these inconsistencies would have to be torturously wrestled with as the implications of this "speculative nonsense."

Here is the next dispensation. You will observe that we cannot call it the sixth Dispensation, for reasons that are so wrong, yet Mr. Caesar has been using it to confine obedience to the law to the past, and not even recognizing that the whole dispensational system depreciates the Plan of Salvation. Every time he uses the term "Dispensation of grace", that term in itself is a depreciation of "grace" of salvation.

> *"This is the dispensation of grace and extends from the "cross" to the "crown" for Christ, and from the "descent of the Holy Spirit" to the 'Rapture of the church" at the Second coming of Christ for the believer. This dispensation is a (PARENTHETICAL DISPENSATION) thrown in between the "Dispersion" of Israel,*

and their "Restoration" to their land. The purpose of this dispensation is to gather out a "People for His Name" called THE CHURCH, composed of both Jew and Gentile. This purpose of God was not revealed in the Old Testament Scriptures, and was unknown to the Patriarchs and Prophets. Christ was the first one to hint at it ..." **Ibid.**, p. 39.

There are many, many things wrong with this consequential teaching. Here, this so-called Dispensation of Grace so often spoken of by Evangelicals is not even given a number, but is merely called a "parenthetical" dispensation. Now, what does the word "parenthetical" mean? It comes from the word "parenthesis", it is described in the following way.

"Parenthesis ... explanatory word, phrase, or clause injected into a sentence without affecting its syntactical construction." **The Scribner-Bantam English Dictionary**, p. 656.

Read the dictionary meaning over and over again until you get the sense of what the word means, and then apply the meaning to the Dispensation of Grace and you will see how it is greatly depreciated. The Dispensation of Grace as an interjection into a flowing dispensation that does not affect the flowing Dispensation would mean that this Dispensation of Grace is not so important, but the flowing dispensation that is not affected is the more important one.

What is this important flowing Dispensation? Why, it is the Dispensation of "law". And in the scheme of Dispensationalism, the Dispensation of law which was from the Exodus to the Cross of Christ, was briefly interrupted by the parenthetical dispensation of Grace, and another one, only to be resumed in what is called the "Millennial Dispensation." Do you see how this so-called Dispensation of Grace is trivialized in this speculative scheme?

We are also told in the former quotation from Mr. Larkin's book that this dispensation of Grace or church age was not known to Patriarchs and Prophets nor was it revealed in the Old Testament scriptures. But this statement is to avoid anyone quoting from the Old Testament to show the church of God prophesied as keeping the law- because there are plenty of such scriptures. Better for them to confine all such scriptures to the Jews only.

In this book aforementioned, Mr. Larkin has a long double - paged chart between pages 5 and 6. The name of the chart is "The Mountain Peaks of Prophecy". In this chart, we have an Old Testament prophet on the left-hand side of the left page looking way down to the end of the right-hand page to the right end of the page. Between are a series of mountains and valleys, the prophet only sees the mountain tops, but cannot see the valleys. The prophet sees the mountain peaks of the "Birth of Jesus", "Calvary", "Pentecost", "Antichrist", etc., but he completely misses the "valley of the church" which is the dispensation of grace, and which begins from the outpouring of the Holy Spirit of the day of Pentecost and ends with the secret rapture. Could you now see how outrageous this Dispensational scheme is? Yet Evangelicals often refer to a "Dispensation of Grace" to confine the Law of God to the past so they would not be convicted that they must keep the Sabbath. Yet this Dispensation doctrine is so much "speculative nonsense", and so outrageous to believe yet they do not see this, neither how it mutilates the gospel.

Did not the prophets prophesy of the church? Did not James, the half-brother of Jesus affirm this truth when he said: 'Sim'e-on hath declared how God at the first did visit the Gentiles, to take out of them a people for his name. And to this agree the words of the prophets; as it is written, After this I will return, and will build again the tabernacle of David, which is fallen down; and I will build again the ruins thereof, and I will set it up: That the residue of men might seek after the Lord, and all the Gentiles, upon whom my name is called, saith the Lord, who doeth all these things." Acts 15:14-17. This textual reference made by James was somewhat modified from Amos 9:11,12. And how about so many prophecies written in the book of Isaiah alone? Here are some: Isaiah 2:1-4; Isaiah 6:3; Isaiah 11:9-12; Isaiah 25:7; Isaiah 44:3-5; Isaiah 45:22; (Isaiah 8:22; Isaiah 9;1,2); Isaiah 49:6,8,9,12; Isaiah 52:6,7,10; Isaiah 54:2,3; Isaiah 56:3,6-8; Isaiah 60:1-11; Isaiah 66:8-12,19,20.

Now since this "valley of the church" Dispensation of Grace is wrong, then we cannot divide up the history of the earth into dispensations, and thus the Dispensation of Grace is wrong, so we cannot confine the law and sabbath to the Jews alone, thus the church that is saved by grace must keep the law.

As Paul says: "Therefore it is of faith, that is might be by grace ..." Romans 4:16, and; "Do we then make void the law through faith? God forbid: yea, we establish the law." Romans 3:31. If a man does not humble to the spirit of truth in the scriptures and turn from his false doctrines, what more can we do for him? We must never forget that "... the works of the flesh are ... heresies ..." Galatians 5:19,20.

Now we turn to the next Dispensation, still it is not the sixth one, but **another** parenthetical one.

> "Between the "Ecclesiastical Dispensation" [the church age, or dispensation of Grace] and the "Millennial dispensation" there is another PARENTHETICAL DISPENSATION, the DISPENSATION OF JUDGEMENT, during which the "Jew", the "Gentiles", and the "church" are to be judged, not as individuals, but nationally or as bodies." Clarence Larkin, **Dispensational Truth or God's Plan and Purpose in the Ages**, p. 40.

This is the notorious dispensation in which the temple will be rebuilt in Jerusalem and the animal sacrifices, feast days, ceremonial laws, and Levitical priesthood will be restored by the salvific will of the Lord. But the church would then have been raptured and the Spirit withdrawn. The dispensation of Grace whereby we are saved, would have been passed already. God alone knows how anyone can be saved without His Grace or the Holy Spirit in this so called dispensation of judgment. Yet we know that God has always dealt with judgments to an impenitent world from the days of the flood even up to this day, thus what judgment needs a dispensation? Let us quickly pass all this nonsense. The next dispensation we come to is called:

> "This is a "Dual Age" and includes the "Millennial Age" and the "Perfect Age", between which the earth is to be "Renovated by Fire"." **Ibid.**, p. 41.

This dispensation is a combination of two "ages", the "Millennial Age" or the thousand years reign of Jews upon the earth while the church is in heaven, and the "Perfect Age" with the eternal new earth set up. The first is called the "Messianic Dispensation" and the latter is called the "Perfect Dispensation". It makes no sense going into the complicated confusion and ludicrousness of the claims of this "Dual Age" which is made up of two dispensations. It is enough to see that, whereas a dispensation was called an "age" before by Mr. Larkin, now he makes the two different by saying that two dispensations fit into one "Age". What justifiable summary could we now make of this dispensational theory? Here the phrase of Mr. Norton when confronted with Darby's Dispensationalism is perfect, it is simply "speculative nonsense".

Now what does the word "dispensation" mean? It is taken from the Greek word "oikonomia" and means "...management of a household;

task, work, responsibility; (divine) plan ..." Barclay M. Newman, Jr., **A Concise Greek-English Dictionary of the New Testament**, p. 124.

The word is further explained:

> *"The Greek words, used about twenty times in the NT, mean "to manage, regulate, administer, and plan the affairs of a household." This concept of human stewardship is illustrated in Luke 16:1-2, where the ideas of responsibility, accountability, and the possibility of change are detailed. In other occurrences (Eph. 1:10; Eph. 3:2,9; Col. 1:25) the idea of divine stewardship is prominent - i.e., an administration or plan being accomplished by God in this world."* Walter A. Elwell, editor, **Evangelical Dictionary of Theology**, p. 321.

We see here that the word "oikonomia" translated "Dispensation" in the Bible should really be translated "house administration" or "administration". It means God's administration to the sinful world, and we know that it is an "administration" of grace, because: "...where sin abounded, grace did much more abound." Romans 5:20. Sin did not abound from the cross of Christ or from the day of Pentecost, so that, grace has not been relevant only from that time so that we can have a dispensation (administration) of grace from the cross or day of Pentecost only to some rapture. Sin was from Adam's time, and so, grace was needed from that moment till now or till the end, for we are all saved by Grace. (Ephesians 2:5) This cuts through all the speculative "Dispensations" and gives us one "administration of Grace" from Adam to the end of the world. For this is exactly what the Scriptures teach: "Wherefore, as by one man sin entered into the world, and death by sin; and so death passed upon all men, for that all have sinned:" Romans 5:12. Thus we have sin existing in an unbroken line from Adam to today. And what has been the answer from Adam to today? Read: "That as sin hath reigned unto death, even so might grace reign through righteousness unto eternal life by Jesus Christ our Lord." Romans 5:21; and Christ is the lamb slain (in God's experience) from the foundation of the world (Revelation 13:8), so that as sin and death has reigned from Adam to today, so grace has reigned giving us Righteousness through the Faith of Jesus Christ (Galatians 2:16). This is why Abel was righteous by Faith (Hebrews 11:4), Noah was righteous by faith (Hebrews 11:7) and all the Old Testament saints that Paul referred to in Hebrews 11. Read the whole chapter. Certainly, all this cuts into these fictitious "Dispensations" rendering them void or as Mr. Norton called them "speculative nonsense". None of the Scriptures where "oikonomia" has been translated "dispensation" in the KJV gives even the slightest references to "ages" or "dispensations" as periods where God deals with a people with a different Plan of Salvation, or any plan for that matter apart from Grace. All one has to do is to read all the scriptures where "dispensation" has been used and substitute it with the word "administration", and immediately, the scales of deception about the ages fall off.

Let us take an example with the text where "dispensation of Grace" has been used to see how it is not speaking about a period of Grace of

ARE EVANGELICALS TRUE BORN AGAIN CHRISTIANS?

Pentecost to any rapture or any such thing at all as Mr. Caesar himself has been using it. We will substitute the word "administration" for "dispensation". Here is it. "If ye have heard of the "administration" of the grace of God which is given me to you-ward:" Ephesians 3:2. All Paul is saying here is that he was given by God the administration of his Grace to the Ephesians, and this is the "Gospel of Grace" (Acts 20:24), as can be seen in the following verse: "How that by revelation he made known unto me the mystery..." Ephesians 3:3. What mystery? Why, the mystery of the gospel, of course. Here is this point seen a little later. "And for me, that utterance may be given unto me, that I may open my mouth boldly, to make known the mystery of the gospel, For which I am an ambassador in bonds: that therein I may speak boldly, as I ought to speak." Ephesians 6:19,20. And you can read Acts 20:24 for the same concept also. In all you will-observe that all "dispensation" means is to "administer" and Paul is administering the gospel of grace. This is what all Old Testament prophets did, even as Noah was a preacher of Righteousness (2 Peter 2:5). Thus, the theory of dispensations falls flat as a lot of "speculative nonsense". The teaching of dispensationalism nevertheless has with it many, many heresies so outrageous that the average believer in it would be appalled to know just what they are believing.

Here are a few, just as a shock therapy.

"In brief... the teachings of dispensationalism are as follows:

1. *The Jews are to be saved by repentance; they are to be left here on earth as God's earthly people.*

2. *The gentiles are to be saved by faith; they will be taken to heaven after the rapture.*

3. *The church is a parenthesis in God's plan and will end in apostasy.*

4. *The kingdom of heaven and the kingdom of God are sharply differentiated, the first being the Davidic kingdom and the latter being God's universal world-wide kingdom.*

5. *God deals with men according to seven dispensations."*
   William E. Cox, **An Examination of Dispensationalism**, p. 8.

And if you cannot see the horror of those teachings perhaps this will add to your shock therapy.

> *"During the millennium, according to dispensationalists, the church will have a position inferior to that of Israel. They teach that, after the millennium, the church will be returned to heaven the second time, there to spend eternity while Israel remains forever on the earth."* **Ibid.**, p. 9.

Look up your Bible in Revelation 21 and 22; is that what the Bible teaches? Certainly not! Then why believe in this dispensationalism? We still have not yet presented its most outrageous teachings that attack the death of Christ and the nature of conversion, but what has been presented is sufficient enough to conclude like Mr. Norton that dispensationalism, as such, is just so much "speculative nonsense".

CHAPTER 6
EVANGELICALS' FALSE JUSTIFICATION DOCTRINE

nother teaching of the Evangelical churches that cuts away at spirituality and has made them depend so much on emotionalism (which they call the Holy Spirit, but which is in fact excitement and emotionalism), is their idea of Justification.

Imagine, on television there is this minister preaching about justification; he proceeds to show the people that God puts His robe of Righteousness on the believer. Then He takes off his jacket and covers a man in front of the audience stating that Christ covers your filthy rags with His pure, clean and white robe of righteousness, and, he adds: "You don't even have to bathe!"

He was so deluded, and deluded an audience of thousands who stood up to cheer him for what he said. But all this was not Biblical in the least way for the Bible explains it this way: "Now Joshua was clothed with filthy garments, and stood before the angel. And he answered and spake unto those that stood before him, saying, take away the filthy garments from him. And unto him he said, behold, I have caused thine iniquity to pass from thee, and I will clothe thee with change of raiment.

And I said, let them set a fair mitre upon his head, and clothed him with garments. And the angel of the Lord stood by." Zechariah. 3:3-5.

Here the Bible clearly teaches that the filthy garments must **first** be removed from the man, then and only then could it be substituted with the robe of Christ's Righteousness. Also, the removing of the filthy garments was explained as the man's "iniquity", which according to the Hebrew text is better translated "perversity", being made to pass, or being removed from him.

The perversity of man is his "carnal mind". "For to be carnally minded is death... Because the carnal mind is enmity against God: for it is not subject to the law of God, neither indeed can be. So then they that are in the flesh cannot please God." Romans 8:6-8. What is needed is a new mind, a spiritual mind; this is being clothed with the robe of Righteousness. "... to be spiritually minded is life ..." Romans 8:6, and "... the Spirit is life because of righteousness." Romans 8:10. Thus to have life is to have the Spirit or righteousness, and to have life is to have the spiritual mind.

How does one receive the spiritual mind or life? Romans 5:18 says it; by the "...justification of life." This tells us that justification gives us life which is the spiritual mind, a substitute for the carnal mind, man's perversity or iniquity which is the filthy garments that must first be dealt with. Thus the robe of righteousness is not a robe that covers man outwardly by proxy, or a robe that covers sin in the life. It is the spiritual mind, the righteousness in the heart.

In Isaiah, this is presented as such: "Hearken unto me, ye that know righteousness, the people in whose heart is my law:" Isaiah 51:7. Which law? "For we know that the law is spiritual ..." Romans. 7:14. So that the Spiritual law in the heart is righteousness in the heart or life in the heart accomplished through justification. Here in the Bible, in so many ways, justification is shown to be a subjective change, a change of mind as David said:

> *"Create in me a clean (Heb. pure) heart, o God; and renew a right spirit within me." Psalm 51:10; or if you prefer, let's look at it as Ezekiel presents it. "A new heart also will I give you, and a new spirit will I put within you: and I will take away the stony heart (the filthy garments) out of your flesh, and I will give you an heart of flesh (robe of righteousness): and I will put my spirit within you ..." Ezekiel 36: 26,27.*

In the light of these scriptures, how can any Evangelical minister, like the preacher on television, present such an erroneous doctrine and expect to be born again or the members of his church to be born again? If a church member was to think that he has some sort of a covering of righteousness while he is yet in his filthy garments of an unclean carnal mind, or while he is yet subjectively unchanged, will he not harbor sins and yet call himself "born again"?

Will he not think that while he is in the experience of sin that he is viewed by God as righteous? Will this not make him have a form of godliness but be absent of the power thereof? This is the terrible state of affairs in Evangelical churches because of a false justification doctrine that they now hold, and one that has strayed from the Reformation concept as taught by Martin Luther.

Here is an account of the Evangelical's false justification doctrine:

> *"He is justified. A man called Bildad once asked the most baffling of questions, 'How then can a man be righteous before God?' (Job 25:4). How can it ever be possible for man to be declared "not guilty" by God when he was born a sinner and is guilty of a life of sin? Look at it the other way, how can God punish sin and yet reverse sentence on the sinner, declaring him free from his guilt? Only God could provide an answer, and he did so in the life and death of Jesus Christ acting as man's substitute. When God declares a man righteous in his sight, he does so on the basis of the life and death of the One who was acting on his behalf... This is beyond our understanding."* John Blanchard, **Right With God**, p. 84.

You would observe that "justified" is made synonymous with "not guilty", or declared "free from guilt", but it does not even touch the man's moral state. Is this biblical justification? No, not at all. We continue:

> *"In explaining the meaning of 'justified', somebody once said that it was 'to be 'just-as-If'-I'd never sinned': yet it means even more than that. When a man is declared by God to be justified, God not only counts him as being 'Not Guilty', but as being righteous in his*

sight. The justified man is treated by God as being one with Christ and therefore all the work of Christ belongs to him as though it was his own work."

"The benefits of Christ's death are his and so also are those of his life. The death of Christ deals with the penalty of all his disobedience, while Christ's righteousness-his conformity to all his Father's perfect will- is the righteousness reckoned by God to belong to each believer. In the matter of our punishment, God looks on the death of Christ and says: 'It is sufficient': in the matter of our acceptance, God looks on the obedience of Christ and says 'I am satisfied'. As a result, the sinner is not only spared the punishment but is brought into fellowship with God. He is not only acquitted from the bar of the courtroom he is welcomed into the heart of the family as a child of God." **Ibid.**, pp. 84-85.

Observe that in this lengthy statement we have quoted, not even in one instance is a change of heart referred to, the carnal mind is not yet taken away, the sinfulness in the mental experience is not removed, yet the believing man is welcomed into the heart of the family as a child of God. All that has happened is that he is declared "not guilty", he is seen **as if** he is righteous in God's sight, but he is not changed internally; in fact all the righteous deeds of Christ are reckoned as his own, the penalty that came upon Christ is esteemed as his own, thus he has escaped the death penalty, but never even once is his moral state referred to.

Is this sensible justice? Is believing enough to make us escape penalty while we are yet unchanged? Is this the gospel of Justification by Faith that was preached by Martin Luther at the beginning of the reformation? Let us look at this false concept from a clearer explanation:

> *'Imputation does not change one's nature; it only affects one's legal standing ... Jesus Christ lived a perfect life-He completely kept God's law. The personal righteousness worked out by Christ during His life on earth is imputed to the sinner the moment he believes. The believer is credited with Christ's righteousness and God views him as if he had done all the good that Christ did. Christ's obedience, His merit, His personal righteousness is imputed to (credited to, set to the account of) the believer's nature (any more than the imputation of sin to Christ changed His nature); it only affects the believer's legal standing before God."* David N. Steele and Curtis C. Thomas, **Romans An Interpretive Outline**, p. 30.

You would observe that the authors plainly state that justification does not make the receiver different. His nature (moral character) is still sinful, yet because he believes, God puts all that Christ ever did to the person's account, so it is as if he did it, and frees the man from penalty for sin, yet he is unchanged. Here is a plain testimony that Evangelicals teach a justification in sin and not from sin. Let us see again the same book.

> *"These expressions mean that believers, through their identification with Christ, are dead to the GUILT of sin. They are*

*viewed by God **as if** they themselves **died** in the **death of Christ** and suffered the full penalty of sin's guilt. Sin can no longer make any legal claim on them; thus, they are **dead** to it-free from its condemnation. That believers are **not dead** to the **influence** or **power** of sin in their lives is proved by the Bible...and Christian experience... It exclusively indicated the justification of believers, and their freedom from the **guilt** of sin, having no allusion to their sanctification...*"**Ibid.**, p. 46.

"Because of His death on the cross, Christ's people are justified (freed from the condemnation of sin) in this life and shall be glorified (freed from the presence and influence of sin) in the life to come." **Ibid.**, p. 48.

"Like Paul, every true believer struggles with indwelling sin ... No believer is able to understand why he sins, it is a mystery beyond his reach... Every believer is assured of deliverance from indwelling sin through Christ Jesus, but not while living in this body of sin." **Ibid.**, pp. 60-61.

"Although the believer is plagued with indwelling sin, his sin can never condemn him. Chapter seven ends with the solemn fact that we are still sinners even after we have been saved (born again); but chapter eight opens with the wonderful assurance that "there is therefore now no condemnation for those who are in Christ Jesus." Those in Christ are justified on the ground of His righteousness which has been imputed to them. In this blessed- truth believers

should find hope and comfort to help them in their fight against sin. They have more than sufficient reason to rejoice; their Lord has already delivered them from the condemning power of sin and will in the resurrection, deliver them from the presence of indwelling sin ... Paul looked for deliverance from indwelling sin but not while in the flesh, and neither can we!" **Ibid.**, p. 61.

Could anything be more shocking to read than these horrible teachings of Evangelicalism? So, while many of them sing and rejoice saying: "Jesus saved me from sin, Jesus set me free", they do not mean an actual freedom from the presence of sin nor the removal of a sinful experience. They either mean just a removal of penalty while remaining in sin, or a future removal of sin from in the heart at the resurrection.

This is salvation by holy flesh. Since for them Justification is not an inner change, but only a deliverance from penalty, and righteousness being placed on some fictitious (or heavenly) account, God could only see them **as if** they are actually righteous, but they are not really so. The average unconverted man can see that he is not yet changed or actually righteous, but God has chosen to blind His eye to the believer's actual present state and feign that the man is righteous when he is in fact not so.

Furthermore; poor God! He is so much against sin, yet He could not furnish a workable plan that would give men victory over sin while in this flesh. How weak was He that sin is too hard for Him to handle in our flesh! No wonder why Evangelicals teach that Christ came in a flesh different from ours, and we wonder therefore, what type of people He came to save.

All this shows us that our true idea of Justification will carry us far up the moral ladder to either be free from indwelling sin at Justification and learn to be maintained that way in sanctification, which is the real teaching of the Bible, or we remain in the experience of sin while thinking we have escaped its penalty and will be delivered from its experience or presence only in the resurrection when we are given a new holy flesh body. This is the false teaching.

Obviously, this will make us live as we please while pinning hope on the fact that we believe, as if that is really any virtue. The devils also believe James 2:19. Of course obedience to God's Law will be under-rated since no one can stop sinning, and this leads to antinomianism. The Sabbath which no one can keep except he is made free from indwelling sin, will be hated because it takes away the false carnal security in sin when its obligation to be kept is set home to the conscience by expository preaching.

Seventh-day Adventists who advocate obedience to the Laws of God and Sabbath-keeping through the Faith of Jesus Christ will be slandered as "legalists", as being "righteous by works", or as a "cult." But all these false labels, and all the anti-law and anti-sabbatarian theology of men like Mr. Caesar and Mr. Johnson are just the carnal mind seeking to justify its presence or existence in the "form-of-godliness-without-the-power".

It is because their theology is twisted that they mutilate the Bible. It is merely the experience of sin or the carnal mind seeking to legitimize its existence in a so called justified man. Thus the problem stems in a large way from the false idea of justification.

Observe again the false justification.

> "Justification relates to man's position, not his condition ... To justify is to set forth as righteous. It is to declare one righteous in a legal sense. It does not deal directly with character or conduct, but with guilt and punishment." Judson Cornwall, **Let us Enjoy Forgiveness**, p. 77.

Do you see how the wide range of Evangelicals all teach the same false justification doctrine not supported in the Bible, neither taught by Luther in the Reformation? Let us look at a final author that is equally erroneous in his understanding of this pivotal doctrine.

> "It is not regeneration, the impartation of life Christ; for although it is "justification of life"-meaning God will give life to the justified, he is justified as **ungodly**...It is not a "new heart", or "change of heart", indefinite expressions at best, but having in them no proper definition of justification...It is not "making an unjust man just" in his life and behavior. The English word **justified** as we all know, comes from the Latin word meaning to snake just or righteous; but this is exactly what justification is **not**, in scripture." William R Newell, **Romans Verse By Verse**, pp. 159-160.

So now that we have laid out what Evangelicals teach concerning Justification, it is now time for us to go back to the beginning of the Lutheran Reformation and search Luther's writings to find out what he taught Justification to be. One thing we know for sure, he never taught the errors we have just read from an assortment of Evangelical authors.

Luther was used by God to discover the true doctrine of Justification that had been buried by Rome, and when he did, it sparked a reformation back towards apostolic Christianity such as never was witnessed before his time. Now what has Luther taught concerning Justification? Was it what is taught today in Evangelical circles? By no means! Let us read from his own writings as to what constitutes justification.

He says:

> "If the law was from the body, it could be satisfied with works; but since it is spiritual, not one can satisfy it, unless all that you do is done from the bottom of the heart. But such a heart is given only by God's Spirit, who makes a man equal to the law, so that he acquires a desire for the law in his heart, and henceforth does nothing out of fear and compulsion, but everything out of a willing heart. That law then is spiritual, which will be loved and fulfilled with such a spiritual heart, and requires such a spirit. Where that spirit is not in the heart, there sin remains, and displeasure with the law and enmity towards it; though the law is good and just and holy."
> Martin Luther, **Commentary on Romans,** p. xiv.

95

Isn't this lovely? You can almost swear that it is a Seventh-day Adventist speaking, but this is exactly what Luther taught. You would observe that he shows us how the Spirit makes our heart love the law of God, and fulfil it. Also, if the spirit is in the heart, no sin remains there. This shows us that justification constitutes a change in the heart so that it loves the Law of God.

Now, Mr. Evangelical, judge yourself in honesty with Luther's Reformation teaching.

> "This pleasure and love for the law is put into the heart by the Holy Ghost, as he says in chapter 5. But the Holy Ghost is not given except in, with and by faith in Jesus Christ... Hence it comes that faith alone makes righteous and fulfills the law; for out of Christ's merits, it brings the Spirit, and the Spirit makes the heart glad and free, as the law requires that it shall be." **Ibid.**, p. xv.

Here the law is put into the heart by the Spirit who is given in faith which makes righteous, thus the subject of the discussion is righteousness by faith or justification; and it is seen to be a subjective work, a work of the Spirit in the heart as said by Luther.

We have here none of the erroneous doctrines like "freedom from penalty" with "no moral change" as we read earlier from the Evangelical. Luther is strictly subjective.

> "And the scripture look especially into the heart and have regard to the root and source of all sin, which is unbelief in the inmost heart.

As, therefore, faith alone makes righteous, and brings the spirit,
and produces pleasure in good, eternal words... **Ibid.**, p. xv-xvi.

"Faith, however, is a divine work in us. It changes us and makes us
to be born anew of God...it kills the old Adam and makes altogether
different men, in heart and spirit, and mind and powers, and it
brings with it the Holy Ghost." **Ibid.**, p. xvii.

Do you not see from these statements of Luther that justification
by faith removes the innermost root of sin in us-the carnal mind, or the
old Adam, and changes us, makes us born anew from God and makes
us different people inwardly? This is what we teach. Now let us hear
Luther again.

"Pray God to work faith in you; else you will remain forever without
faith, whatever you think or do. Righteousness, then, is such a faith
and is called "God's righteousness", or "the righteousness that
avails before God," because God gives it and counts it as
righteousness for the sake of Christ, our Mediator, and makes a
man give to every man what he owes him. For through faith a man
becomes sinless and comes to take pleasure in God's
commandments; thus he gives to God the honor that is His and
pays Him what he owes him..." **Ibid.**, p. xvii.

Notice that Luther says: "... through faith a man becomes sinless...",
certainly this is a different justification to what is taught by
Evangelicals today, who believe that in the justifying of a man his

97

experience of sin still remains. Evidently, Evangelicals of today do not have the same gospel that Luther started the reformation with. We continue.

> "On the other hand, if Abraham's circumcision was an external sign by which he showed the righteousness that was already his in faith, then all good works are only external signs which follow out of faith, and show, like good fruit, that man is already inwardly righteous before God." **Ibid.**, p. xx.

Thus all good works done in faith which gives righteousness, shows that we are already inwardly righteous before God and that justification by faith is being made inwardly righteous, and this causes us to have good works, the fruit of being inwardly righteous.

Luther even proceeds to show justification as the new spiritual birth.

> "He says that Christ had to come, a second Adam, to bequeath His righteousness to us through a new spiritual birth in faith, as the first Adam bequeathed sin to us, through the old, fleshly birth." **Ibid.**, p. xxi.

> "... the spirit comes from Christ, who has given us His Holy Spirit to make us spiritual and subdue the flesh." **Ibid.**, p. xxiii.

All this shows that even though we are in this flesh, we can **overcome** sin and do not have to wait for a new holy body to be free from the power of sin. Justification is the change from sin into righteousness. It is separation from sin unto holiness that our sanctification may continue.

In Martin Luther's preface of his **Commentary on Romans** printed in 1552 A.C.B., no way presents justification as just freedom from penalty, or a proxy righteousness being placed on some heavenly account, that we are seen as righteous while sin is still alive within us. No! He presents justification as a change of heart, a new spiritual birth, the gift of the Holy Spirit, and the making of man inwardly righteous. Years later, when John Wesley read it, he became converted. Conversion for him meant a change of heart, for that was how he understood justification in Luther's **Commentary on Romans.** Here is what Wesley said:

> *"In the evening I went very unwillingly to a society in Aldersgate Street, where one was reading Luther's Preface to the Epistle to the Romans. About a quarter before nine, while he was describing the change which God works in the heart through faith in Christ. I felt my heart strangely warmed. I felt I did trust in Christ, Christ alone, for my salvation; and an assurance was given me that He had taken my sins away, even mine, and saved me from the law of sin and death."* **Journal of John Wesley**, May 24, 1738.

Thus justification is in fact a change of heart, let us **never** forget that, and to this end we shall give a series of quotations from another of

Luther's quotations to prove that he did in fact teach a subjective justification.

> "...this one solid rock which we call the doctrine of justification. I mean the doctrine that we are redeemed from sin, death and the devil, and made partakers of eternal life, not by ourselves (and certainly not by our works, which are less than ourselves), but by the help of another, the only-begotten Son of God, Jesus Christ." Martin Luther, **A Commentary on St. Paul's Epistle to the Galatians (1575 Edition)** p. 16.

> "There is yet another righteousness which is above all these: to wit, the righteousness of faith, or christian righteousness... But this most excellent righteousness, of faith I mean (which God through Christ, without works, imputeth unto us), is neither political nor ceremonial, nor the righteousness of God's law, nor consisteth in our works, but is clean contrary: that is to say, a mere passive righteousness, as the other above are active. For in this we work nothing, we render nothing unto God, but only we receive and suffer another to work in us, that is to say, God. Therefore it seemeth good unto me to call this righteousness of faith or christian righteousness, the passive righteousness." **Ibid., p.** 22.

Isn't this lovely? Here Luther calls righteousness by faith the work of God "in us". This is clear proof for a subjective justification.

Let us look again at more proof.

"But this righteousness is heavenly and passive: which we have not of ourselves, but receive it from heaven: which we work not, but apprehend it by faith: whereby we mount up above all laws and works. Wherefore like as we have borne (as St Paul saith) the image of the earthly Adam, so let us bear the image of the heavenly (1 Corinthians 15:49), which is the new man in a new world, where is no law, no sin, no sting of conscience, no death, but prefect joy, righteousness, grace, peace, life, salvation and glory. Why do we then do nothing? Do we work nothing for the obtaining of this righteousness? I answer: Nothing at all. For the nature of this righteousness is, to do nothing, to hear nothing, to know nothing whatsoever of the law or of works, but to know and to believe this only, that Christ is gone to the Father and is not now seen: that he sitteth in heaven at the right hand of his Father, not as a judge, but made unto us of God, wisdom, righteousness, holiness and redemption: briefly, that he is our high-priest entreating for us, and reigning over us and in us by grace. Here no sin is perceived, no terror or remorse of conscience is felt; for in this heavenly righteousness sin can have no place..." **Ibid.**, p. 25.

Read the statement all over again until you understand it carefully; isn't it beautiful? The basic points to note are that justification is the gift of a heavenly righteousness that is not by our works. It is bearing the "image of the heavenly" which is the "new man". It is Christ reigning "in us", and thus no sin is there. This isn't what Evangelicals teach today.

No! Not at all, yet this teaching of Luther that the reformation began with is the true justification.

> *"... for I am baptized and by the gospel am called to the partaking of righteousness and of everlasting life, to the kingdom of Christ, ... for I will not suffer thee, so intolerable a tyrant and cruel tormentor, to reign in my conscience, for it is the seat and temple of Christ the Son of God, who is the king of righteousness and peace, and my most sweet saviour and mediator: he shall keep my conscience joyful and quiet in the sound and pure doctrine of the gospel, and in the knowledge of this passive and heavenly righteousness. When I have this righteousness reigning in my heart, I descend from heaven as the rain making fruitful the earth..."* **Ibid.**, p. 28.

Here the righteousness reigns in the heart. The conscience is the seat and dwelling place of Christ, all this reveals that justification is indeed subjective. Here is more evidence:

> *"Faith therefore justifieth, because it apprehendeth and possessseth this treasure, even Christ present...Wherefore, where assured trust and affiance of the heart is, there Christ is present, yea even in the cloud and obscurity of faith. And this is the true formal righteousness, whereby a man is justified...Wherefore Christ apprehended by faith, and dwelling in the heart, is the true Christian righteousness, for the which God counteth us righteous and giveth us eternal life."* **Ibid.**, p. 135.

"This is the beginning of health and salvation. By this means we are delivered from sin, justified and made inheritor of everlasting life; not for our own works and deserts, but for our faith, whereby we lay hold upon Christ. Wherefore we also do acknowledge a quality and a formal righteousness in the heart..." **Ibid.**, p. 136.

Could anything be clearer than that? Luther says that a quality and a formal righteousness is in the heart when a man is justified by faith. Here is Luther again.

"Here is to be noted, that these three things, faith, Christ, acceptation, or imputation, must be joined together. Faith taketh hold of Christ, and hath him present, and holdeth him enclosed, as the ring doth the precious stone. And whosoever shall be found having this confidence in Christ apprehended in the heart, him God will account for righteous." **Ibid.**, p. 137.

Observe this revealing statement.

"In him we are by faith, and he in us." **Ibid.**, p. 142.

Here again is another "in-ness" quotation that shows the subjectivity of justification.

"Here we ourselves must be nothing at all, but only receive the treasure which is Christ, apprehended in our hearts by faith..." **Ibid.**, p. 143.

"Christ therefore, saith he, thus joined and united unto me and abiding in me, liveth this life in me which now I live; yea, Christ himself, is this life which now I live. Wherefore Christ and I in this behalf are both one." **Ibid.**, p. 168.

"... but as concerning justification, Christ and I must be entirely co-joined and united together, so that he may live in me and I in him. And this is a wonderful manner of speech. Now because Christ liveth in me, therefore what-so-ever of grace, righteousness, life, peace and salvation is in me, it is all his, and yet notwithstanding the same is mine also, by that inseparable union and conjunction, which is through faith; by the which Christ and I are made as it were one body in spirit. Forasmuch then as Christ liveth in me, it followeth that as there must needs be present with him, grace, righteousness, life and eternal salvation..." **Ibid.**, p. 169.

Now observe how united we ought to be with Christ when we are justified. Here Luther says:

"If therefore in the matter of justification thou separate the person of Christ from thy person, then art thou in the law, thou abidest in it, and livest in thyself and not in Christ, and so thou art condemned of the law, and dead before God." **Ibid.**, p. 169-170.

Of course, when Luther says "thou art in the law" he does not mean in "obedience" to the law, but merely in the works of the law without Christ. This is why he says that the person "livest in thyself and not in Christ" and why also he is "condemned of the law". But the idea of the close union of Christ and the justified person is emphatic here as in the following statement.

> *"Faith therefore must be purely taught: namely, that by faith thou art so entirely and nearly joined unto Christ, that he and thou are made as it were one person; so that thou mayest boldly say: 1 am now one with Christ, that is to say, Christ is righteousness, victory and life are mine."* **Ibid.**, p. 170.

Here are some more lovely quotations from Luther on the subjectivity of justification:

> *"Natural motion is our motion, but the movement of justification is the work of God in us, to which our positions refer."* **Disputation on Justification** (1536) Quoted in, Erwin R. Cane, **The Scriptural Doctrine of Justification**, pp. 13-14.

Observe how clear that truth is; and whenever Luther says the righteousness of God is outside of us, what does he mean? Does he mean it is not in us? No, he explains himself.

> *"The phrase is grammatical. To be outside of us means not to be out of our powers. Righteousness is our possession, to be sure, since it was given to us out of mercy. Nevertheless, it is foreign to us because we have not merited it."* **Ibid.**, p. 14.

This is as far as we will go in proving that Luther did teach a justification that removes the carnal mind or experience of sin from within the man, and substitutes it with the Holy Spirit, Christ dwelling within, righteousness within, a changed heart, a new man, the new birth and many other realities. Suffice to say, he never taught any Evangelical nonsense of waiting for the resurrection to be free from the actual presence of sin within, while God only sees us **as if** we are righteous.

Now the next quest we have is to find out who or what caused the change of the true doctrine of justification by faith, so that today evangelicalism now espouses a false concept which Luther never taught.

Our research takes us to Melanchthon, Luther's helper and friend in the reformation, and who took over from Luther when he died. Let's read what Carl E. Braaten says:

> 'It Was Melanchthon, who made the great mistake of narrowing justification down to the declaration that sinners are righteous on account of the external merits of Christ, whereas Luther allegedly understood justification as a real transformation of persons from the state of sinfulness to that of righteousness." Carl E. Braaten, **Justification**, p. 13.

Mr. Braaten is speaking about a Mr. Karl Holl's claim as a result of his studies in Luther's theology. Karl Holl was not only the "... pioneer of modern Luther studies ..." he was also the most thorough of all in such research. Braaten sums up what Holl taught as a result of his Luther studies:

"For Holl, God does not only declare a person righteous, he literally makes a person righteous." **Ibid.**, p. 13.

Thus we see that while Luther taught a subjective change- creating justification, it was his friend Melanchthon who gradually introduced a change in the doctrine until it was presented as strictly forensic, and as not relating to a person's moral experience as is taught by evangelicalism today. Therefore, Evangelicals' justification doctrine comes not from Luther's teaching, but from a change of his teaching that occurred somewhere in the middle of the sixteenth century. Mr. Walter F. Bense says of Mr. Holl:

"Holl points out elsewhere that it was Melanchthon who assumed, and taught a whole generation of lutheran clergymen (if not all Lutheranism) to assume, that religion necessarily aims at blessedness. But according to Holl this assumption would give up one of Luther's greatest accomplishments; namely, the consistent elaboration of a religion that teaches one to assume full responsibility for oneself, simultaneously to recognize that all one has is God's free gift, and above all, to participate (in a kind of active passivity or passive activity) in God's transformation of one's self, of others and of the world itself." Editor's introduction to: Karl Holl, **What Did Luther Understand by Religion?** pp. 3- 4.

What we are being told is that, it was Melanchthon who taught a whole generation of Lutheran theologians with his false justification that emphasized the aim of true religion to be just "blessedness", in an objective sense. This caused the loss within lutheranism and consequentially the whole reformation, of Luther's true justification doctrine which emphasized God's transformation of the penitent and led to personal moral responsibility.

Let's hear Mr. Karl Holl himself speaking about the ills of Melanchthon's teachings:

> "In Luther's thinking, the death of Christ is intimately connected with his resurrection. "His resurrection from the dead is our justification through faith alone" (**Drews Disputaionen**, p. 732. thesis 2). Here Luther counteracts the one-sidedness characteristic of Western theology since the time of Anselm, which also overtook later Lutheran theology under Melanchthon's influence-namely, the idea that the death of Christ is the one great fact of salvation. Luther revives the Pauline view that death and the resurrection constitute an inseparable unity." **Ibid.**, pp. 76-77.

This is a most significant revelation on the part of Mr. Holl. If as Evangelicals teach, the death of Christ paid our penalty and thus becomes our deliverance from death, and sin in the believing one is in no way eradicated by the death on the cross, then not only will we have to wait until the resurrection and gift of a new body to remove the presence of sin from in our experience, but the resurrection of Christ is given no consequence here. So it makes no sense to teach that Christ resurrected and ascended into the heavenly sanctuary to minister the merits of His salvation to us, like for example, justification. Evangelicals' theology is therefore a theology of death and not of life.

Mr. Holl continues to speak:

> *"To put it differently, Luther regards faith as a coming to grips not only with the guilt of sin but also with its power. This is essential. Only because he can trust in a divine power that purges him of sin does Luther have a "clear conscience", and sin, death, and the devil are really vanquished for him. We see here how unjust it is to regard Luther's faith as mere "comfort in the misery of sin" [as Melanchthon taught], and on this basis to give an advantage to Calvin [who taught the false justification, and once saved always saved]. The slogan of mere "comfort in the misery of sin" applies only to Lutheran Orthodoxy (influenced by Melanchthon), not to Luther himself."* **Ibid.**, p. 77.

Thus Evangelicals' justification doctrine that does not get rid of sin from within the believer, but makes them trust in an external righteousness on some so called "account", and not in them, and *give* them comfort that they have escaped penalty for sin in the substitutionary death of Christ, is Melanchthon's "comfort in the misery of sin" doctrine and not Luther's teaching. Again, Mr. Holl states:

> *"...This...Melanchthon doctrine of justification ineluctably (unavoidably) leads to the concepts of merit ... In justification, Luther regards it as essential that the one with whom God-out of*

free grace-has entered into relationship will also actually become righteous in this relationship; otherwise God's judgement of justification would amount to a lie. To be sure, it is not a case of forming a good intention to "mend one's ways" after one has been justified; rather, God himself transforms the person within the new relationship ... God's instrument for transforming the person, however, is Christ. For Luther does not look upon Christ simply as the one who has atoned for the sins of humanity by his death but also at the same time as the Risen One, who is alive and at work in the hearts of believers. Luther recovered the meaning of the Pauline unity of the death and resurrection of Christ; but his recovery was slow to bear fruit within Protestantism. Melanchthon was unable to appreciate it, that is why it failed to become part of [Lutheran] Orthodoxy." **Ibid.**, p. 117.

Of course Melanchthon taught a whole generation of Lutherans who influenced the Reformation greatly, thus the false justification doctrine and its attendant errors that lead to anti-nomianism (against God's law) and anti-sabbatarianism took over in the world of Evangelical theology and now reigns. Did you know one of the main reasons why Luther prayed for Melanchthon? It was because even when Luther was yet alive Melanchthon began to shift from the real gospel. Observe:

"This is what Luther did in his famous prayer for Melanchthon. He felt that the issue at this moment was not simply Melanchthon's

personal fate, but that the great cause of the gospel was involved."
Ibid., p. 89.

Indeed it was, and Luther read the future accurately. Thus we assert and affirm that the false justification teaching came from Melanchthon, Luther did not teach that heresy. Mr. Alister E. Mc Grath notes:

> *"However, Luther was no systematic theologian; he preferred to write in response to particular needs, rather than writing theological text books, and the task of consolidating his doctrine of justification was left to others, most notably Philip Melanchthon, who was responsible for drawing up the famous Augsburg confession of 1530. It seems that Luther's doctrine of justification was modified somewhat by his followers, such as Melanchthon..."*
> Alister E. Mc Grath, **Justification By Faith**, p. 55.

What kind of changes did Melanchthon bring concerning the doctrine of Justification by Faith? This author gives us an account that is somewhat partial, but is fair enough to give an idea where Evangelicals get their false justification doctrine. Here is it.

> *"Melanchthon gives the following definition of justification: 'To be justified does not mean that an ungodly man is made righteous, but that he is **pronounced righteous in a forensic manner**." Augustine had interpreted the Latin verb justificare ("to justify") as justum facere ("to make righteous'). But Melanchthon eliminates*

*this idea: justification is about being **declared or pronounced righteous**, not being **made righteous**...In effect, Melanchthon and Calvin distinguish two aspects of the process that both Augustine and the young Luther had treated as a single unit. Thus Augustine taught [as Luther also] that justification embraces all of christian existence, including both the **event** of being treated as righteous and the **process** of becoming righteous. For Melanchthon and Calvin, however, the event (Justification) and the process (sanctification) could be and should be distinguished. The forgiveness of sins and the renewing gift of the Holy Spirit are to be treated as logically distinct."* **Ibid.**, p. 56.

It must however be noted here that Luther taught subjective or a change-producing Justification not only in his youth, but in his old age as we have shown above in numerous of quotations from his writings, and while he did teach that when God "declares a man righteous", He in fact "makes a man righteous", but it is not in the same sacramental sense as Augustine. Also, Luther taught that justification embraces the whole of a Christian's existence from beginning to end. There was a time when Melanchthon questioned Luther on this aspect of the doctrine and Luther gave him an answer in the affirmative. Thus Melanchthon should not have done what he did in his defining of justification that left out the fact that it is indeed a change. Here is a short reference to that conversation between Luther and Melanchthon:

"**Melanchthon**: *When you say: We are justified only by faith, do you understand that only from the beginning of the remission of sins?* **Luther**: *From the beginning, from the middle, and from the end. No piecing or partial cause approaches thereunto: for faith is powerful continually without ceasing, otherwise it is no faith.*"
Quoted from: Horace Bushnell, **The Vicarious Sacrifice Vol. 2**, p. 269.

Thus, for Luther, the change that occurs in justification enthrones Christ in the heart from the beginning, in the middle and to the end, for continual faith must remain in the person to the end if they are to be saved.

"*...according to Luther, Christ comes to dwell within the believer and is involved with his existence internally.*"Alister E. Mc Grath, **Justification by Faith**, p. 57

Melanchthon's change in Luther's doctrine of a change-creating justification influenced the reformer John Calvin who even further developed the doctrine to what is believed today. Calvin grappled with the problems Melanchthon's false justification doctrine created and developed it into such a way that is became an acceptable teaching.

"*It was due to the genius of John Calvin that this difficulty was completely overcome- in fact, so successful was Calvin's solution that it was adopted by just about every Lutheran theologian as well, despite Luther's somewhat different views on the matter."* **Ibid.**, p. 57.

Evangelicals who claim to be born again need to find out the source of their idea of justification. This book presents the facts as they are. Why criticize unjustly the teachings of Adventism, while you have not even researched your own teachings? When Evangelicals teach "Justification by Faith" today, one can clearly observe from whence it came. Observe where these false ideas originated, not from Luther, but from men who perverted what Luther taught.

> *"For the later Reformers, such as Melanchthon and Calvin, the basis of our justification is the righteousness of Christ, earned through his obedience to God in his life and death. This righteousness however, is always alien and external to us: we do not possess in our selves sufficient righteousness upon which the verdict of divine justification may be based. The righteousness of Christ is thus "imputed" to us-in other words, it is treated as if it were ours, or reckoned to us, or reckoned to us without ever becoming ours."* **Ibid.**, p. 59.

But for Luther, when God justifies us He in fact puts His righteousness in us, it is in us for sure; but Luther's use of the phrase that righteousness is "outside of us" merely means that it is not from man's ability or powers that righteousness whereby we are justified comes. That is all he meant and nothing more. Here Luther speaks again.

"The phrase is grammatical. To be outside of us means not to be out of our powers. Righteousness is our possession, to be sure, since it was given to us out of mercy. Nevertheless, it is foreign to us, because we have not merited it." Quoted in Erwin R. Gane, **The Scriptural Doctrine of Justification,** p. 14.

We are now living at the end of the world, and the divisions made by Melanchthon, and then Calvin have fully blossomed into a great, grand worldwide Evangelical movement, but, alas, they only have a form of godliness but deny the power thereof (2 Timothy 3: 5). Thus the following statement is true.

"What the first fifteen hundred years of the Christian church had called "justification" now had to be spilt into two parts, one of which was still called "justification". Alister E. Mc Grath, **Justification by Faith,** p. 59.

We are told of this same thing even clearer by the same author in another of his books. We present the statement for additional emphasis.

"These ideas were subsequently developed by Luther's follower Philip Melanchthon to give the doctrine now generally known as "forensic justification". Where Augustine taught that the sinner is **made righteous** *in justification, Melanchthon taught that he is* **counted as righteous** *or* **pronounced to be righteous.** *For Augustine, "justifying righteousness" is* **imparted:** *for Melanchthon, it is* **imputed.** *Melanchthon drew a sharp*

115

distinction between the event of being declared righteous and the process of being **made** *righteous, designating the former "justification" and the latter "sanctification" or "regeneration". For Augustine, both were simply different aspects of the same thing. According to Melanchthon, God pronounces the divine judgment that the sinner is righteous-in the heavenly court (in foro divino). This legal approach to justification gives rise to the term "forensic justification", from the Latin word* **forum** *("marketplace" or "courtyard)- the place traditionally associated with the dispensing of justice in classical Rome. The importance of this development lies in the fact that it marks a complete break with the teaching of the church up to that point. From the time of Augustine onward, justification had always been understood to refer to both the event of being declared righteous and the process of being made righteous. Melanchthon's concept of forensic justification diverged radically from this. As it was taken up by virtually all the major reformers subsequently, it came to represent a standard difference between the Protestant and Roman Catholic churches from that point onward."* Alister E. Mc Grath, **Christian Theology An Introduction**, p. 387.

Of course Roman Catholicism has a form of subjective justification, but not in the real Biblical sense. They also have an **objective** justification just like the Evangelicals, and also a justification by works. They have everything, but not the Truth, and the quotation given is sufficient enough to show the real origin of the Evangelical's false teaching of justification. Then as the years passed by after Melanchthon, each new generation of theologians took up his concept and carried it yet further and further levelling all good remnants of teaching to their evil forensic justification doctrine. Here is just one small example.

> *"The old view advocated by the Reformers and Puritans, failed by making the whole [dying to sin] too much a subjective experience, or an inward renovation. The origin of the misinterpretation must be traced to the separation of the sixth chapter from the fifth, as if a wholly new subject began at Rom. 6:1. Compare the words of Horatius Bonar, who after having defended Haldane's interpretation, states 'to be dead to sin' is a judicial or legal, not a moral figure. It refers to our release from condemnation, our righteous disjunction from the claim and curse of the laws."* David N. Steele and Curtis C. Thomas, **Romans An Interpretive Outline**, p. 47.

Dying to sin is not deliverance from condemnation, it is absurd to claim so; but the false justification doctrine can be disannulled by many other scriptures which contradict it, and so to keep the doctrine existing, a reinterpretation of those texts has been embarked upon by many theologians, to the extent that today all scriptures that relate to justification are strained to teach, and looked at in the light of the false justification. But there are so many scriptures that teach subjective or change-creating justification. For example Romans 3:22 -the Greek text tells us that the "... righteousness of God which is by faith of Jesus Christ into (eis) all ...); Romans 4:6-8 is clearly drawn from Psalm 32:1,2,5,11 which shows that the justified is "... upright in heart" Justification gives us life and peace according to Romans 8:6; Romans 5:1,18, and this is having a spiritual mind. Romans 6:6 which is evidently subjective is effectively summed up as to be justified in the Greek text of Romans 6:7; it says:

"For he that is dead is justified from the sin" Titus 3:5-7 presents justification as "washing of regeneration" and "renewing of the Holy Ghost", this is also change-creating. Therefore any true doctrine of Justification held, must be that it is subjective or else the movement that holds any other concept is false like it. Evangelicals, be warned! For as the Scriptures said, that without the New Jerusalem is, "...whosoever loveth and maketh a lie." Revelation 22:15.

CHAPTER 7
EVANGELICAL ANTI-NOMIANISM

One of the most nefarious doctrines held by Evangelicals, and one which disqualifies them from being the true church of God is their teaching of "Anti-nomianism". Anti-nomianism is described as such:

> *"The word comes from the Greek "anti" (against) and "nomos"* *(law), and refers to the doctrine that it is not necessary for* *Christians to preach and/or obey the moral law of the O.T."* Walter A. Elwell, Editor, **Evangelical Dictionary of Theology**, p.57.

How could anyone teach that the Law of God, the Ten Commandments, is not binding on anyone to keep? The Bible says that: "Whosoever committeth sin transgresseth also the law: for sin is the transgression of the law." 1 John.3:4. We are also told "...for where no law is, there is no transgression." Romans 4:15, and, "...Is the law sin? God forbid. Nay, I had not known sin, but by the law: for I had not known lust, except the law had said, Thou shalt not covet." Romans 7:7 Also, "...but sin is not imputed when there is no law." Romans 5:13. Jesus came to save us **from** sin not **in** sin because "...thou shalt call his name JESUS: for he shall save his people **from** their sins." Matthew 1:21. This means that in the experience of salvation which Jesus gives to the penitent, there must be deliverance from breaking or transgression of God's law, and one must be brought into obedience to the Commandments. This is why Jesus said: "...if thou wilt enter into life, keep the commandments." Matthew 19:17. He showed this from Psalm which says: "The law of the Lord is perfect converting the soul..." Psalm 19:7. He was explaining which law He meant and did not leave us to guess. He said: "...Thou shalt do no murder, Thou shalt not commit adultery, Thou shalt do not steal, Thou shalt not bear false witness, Honour thy father and thy mother: Thou shalt love thy neighbour as thyself." Matthew 19:18,19.

It is evident that Christ was quoting from the Ten Commandments which He summed up as "Thou shalt love thy neighbour as thyself." Also, the apostle John who leaned on Jesus' bosom (John.13:23) stated clearly: "By this we know that we love the children of God, when we love God, and keep his commandments. For this is the love of God, that we keep his commandments: and his commandments are not grievous." John.5:2,3 and, "And this is love, that we walk after his commandments. This is the commandment, that as ye have heard from the beginning, ye should walk in it." 2 John 6.

All these and many other scriptures confirm that we must keep the law of God. Yet despite this, Evangelical sects have become so hardened in their hate for God's law that they simply choose to overlook these scriptures and some of them cast an interpretation that effectively nullifies their claims.

Evangelicals have a habit of lying on Seventh-Day Adventists in regard to the role of the Law in our salvific life. They continually misrepresent our beliefs on the Law of God. They claim that we are not justified and that we depend on the works of the Law for salvation or to justify ourselves. They set Law and Grace against each other as if they are mortal enemies; they forget that if this was so, then when Law existed there was no Grace at all and vice versa. Many, many books have been written to downplay the role of the Law, yet there is not a shred of scripture that shows Jesus Christ doing this, not even the apostles. Observe what Caesar says:

> *"Then too, since those peculiar Jewish laws aptly called the enmity in Eph. 2:15-16, created a middle wall of partition between the Jews and the Gentiles (Eph. 2:14-16), but are of no spiritual value to the church of Jesus Christ today, Jesus Christ abolished them, by nailing them to his cross..."* Wordsworth N. Caesar, **The Middle Wall of Partition that Jesus Broke Down**, p.22.

Lest someone thinks that Caesar is speaking about the Ceremonial laws of Israel, let him explain himself:

> *"Now from Jesus' treatment of this sabbath issue, linking, as He did, an old ceremonial law with the sabbath (1 Sam. 21:1-6 and Matt. 12:1-8), He provided us with irrefutable proof that He did not divide the law into ceremonial and moral, as we are being told by the S.D.A. (all sects) today..."* **Ibid.**, p.27.

Mr. Caesar by this statement unites the ceremonial law and the moral law as **one**, and since he says that they "...are of no spiritual value to the church of Jesus Christ today, Jesus Christ abolished them...", he is therefore claiming that the moral law was abolished. What else is this but rank anti-nomianism? And it is not only rank anti-nomianism, it is also rank lies. It is the product of a twisted reasoning, one bent against the law of God at all cost, even the cost of Truth. The real truth about the moral law of the Ten Commandments is that it was so different from the ceremonial law that God said through Moses: "These words the Lord spake unto all your assembly in the mount out of the midst of the fire, of the cloud, and of the thick darkness, with a great voice: and he added no more. And he wrote them in two tables of stone, and delivered them unto me." Deuteronomy 5:22.

Here we are told that God "added no more", then as we look upon the two tables of stone, all we shall find is the Ten Commandments and nothing else. We cannot find circumcision or any of the ceremonial sabbaths there, thus they are not to be classed together. But it is convenient for Mr. Caesar to mingle them together by an existential leap of macabre reasoning in his extreme antinomianism and in his covert effort to throw the baby out with the bath water. But again, the scriptures tell us that God wrote the Ten Commandments with His finger. "And the Lord said unto Moses, Come up to me into the mount, and be there: and I will give thee tables of stone, and a law, and commandments which I have written; that thou mayest teach them." Exodus 24:12.

"And he gave unto Moses, when he had made an end of communing with him upon mount Sinai, two tables of testimony, tables of stone, written with the finger of God." Exodus 31:18. "And Moses turned, and went down from the mount, and the two tables of the testimony were in his hand: the tables were written on both their sides; on the one side and on the other were they written. And the tables were the work of God, and the writing was the writing of God, graven upon the tables." Exodus 32:15,16. But the Scriptures also tell us that Moses wrote the Ceremonial Law with his hand.

"And it came to pass, when Moses had made an end of writing the words of this law in a book, until they were finished." Deuteronomy 31:24. Here are circumstances that give us two laws; God wrote one with His finger on stone, it contained Ten Commandments (Deuteronomy 10:4), and He added no more, and Moses wrote all ceremonies in a book called the Book of the Law (Deuteronomy 28:58,61; Deuteronomy 30:10; Deuteronomy 31:24,26). And where were each of them placed? In different places. Of the Ten Commandments on the tables of stone we are told: "And I turned myself and came down from the mount, and put the tables in the ark which I had made; and there they be, as the LORD commanded me" (Deuteronomy 10:5). "That Moses commanded the Levites, which bare the ark of the covenant of the Lord, saying, Take this book of the law and put it in the side of the ark of the covenant of the Lord your God, that it may be there for a witness against thee." Deuteronomy 31:25,26.

Here we see that while the tables of stone on which the Ten Commandments written with the finger of God were placed into the box called the ark, the other laws written by the hand of Moses in a book (or scroll) was placed in pockets in the side of the ark, thus the two were placed in different places making them different. So in different ways the differences between the ceremonial laws which include sacrifices, rituals, holy days and lunar-sabbaths, etc., and the moral law of the Ten Commandments, are clearly stated in the scriptures contrary to what Mr. Caesar claims. No efforts of Mr. Caesar's, or anyone else to trumpet their anti-nomianism will work, for the law of God is to be kept by faith and not just by human works or mere human efforts.

Evangelicals must cease lying on Adventism. Among other falsehoods that Adventism does not teach, yet is accused of are:

a. That we do the works of the law for salvation.

b. That we worship the Sabbath because we sing hymns about the Sabbath.

c. That we are not saved by Grace.

But all this is not true, because Adventism does not do the works of the law to gain salvation. We are in the **experience** of salvation from sin which is transgression of the Law, when we are in **obedience** to the law of God, but not by our works, but through the faith of Jesus Christ which puts the spiritual law or the righteousness of God (His Divine Nature) in us which causes us to do the works of the law. This is a Biblical teaching.

We do indeed believe that it is God's grace that saves us, it is His mercy, kindness and favour that saves us **from** sin, not **in** sin. Grace does not abolish the law or the responsibility of obedience. Grace in fact is to establish law keeping, but from divine initiation in us, not from our own initiation. Also, we do **not** believe that to sing a hymn about the sabbath is to worship that day, just as singing "The Old Rugged Cross" is not worshipping the wooden cross. Yet Evangelicals usually cast up these "straw men", and why? To knock them down again by perverted rational and thus gain scholastic credibility to substantiate their dangerous false doctrines. However, men like Mr. Caesar and Mr. Morris Johnson have gone overboard with their anti-nomianism. Evangelicalism in theory at least is not supposed to be anti-nomian. Observe what this Evangelical dictionary states:

> *"The Christian community as a whole has rejected antinomianism over the years for several reasons. It has regarded the view as damaging to the unity of the Bible, which demands that one part of the divine revelation must not contradict another...In general, orthodoxy teaches that the moral principles of the law are still valid, not as objective striving but as fruits of the Holy Spirit at work in the life of the believer. This disposes of the objection that since the law is too demanding to be kept, it can be completely thrust aside*

as irrelevant to the individual living under grace." Walter A Elwell,
Editor, **Evangelical Dictionary of Theology**, p.59.

People like the two men mentioned above need to take note of the
above statement and work out a theology that includes obedience to the
law of God. Especially should Mr. Caesar take note since he has already
grossly divided the two revelations of the Old and New Testaments
beyond repair. Certainly, we know that Mr. Caesar and Mr. Johnson and
all like them **will** be "called the least in the kingdom of heaven", because
they have broken the Sabbath commandment of God, and have taught
men to do so (see Matthew 5:17-19).

Now let us deal in a bit of history of antinomianism. Remember we
have already explained what that big word really means. In a nutshell
here it is:

> *"Some have taught that once persons are justified by faith in Christ,
> they no longer have any obligation towards the moral law because
> Jesus has freed them from it."* **Ibid.**, pp.57-58.

This teaching has a most corrupt historical past of which we don't
have the space to enter into at this moment. But we are told that this
problem was already in the apostolic church and that Paul had to fight
against it.

> *"For example, there were those in the Corinth church who taught
> that once people are justified by faith, they could engage in
> immorality since there was no longer any obligation to obey the*

moral law (1 Cor.5-6). Paul also had to correct others who obviously
had drawn wrong conclusions from his teachings on justification
and grace..." **Ibid.**, p.58

Subtract the teaching that one "could engage in immorality" and the rest is what Mr. Caesar's book teaches. Of his book **The Middle Wall of Partition that Jesus Christ Broke Down** we can safely say that here is an exceptional book, it is a tortured tissue of lies, a "hodge podge" of glaring contradictions, Satan's snake-winding art of lies and deceptions, yet the author purports to be teaching Pauls' gospel. But Romans 3:31 is the key to understand the role of the Law with respect to keeping it in the writings of Paul. Paul never presents his gospel as antinomian; he may speak against the ceremonial laws (sabbaths included), he may repeat that we are saved by Grace, he may tell us that we are not justified by the works of the Law as our initiative, he may speak of old and new covenants, but none of these things are to be construed that the Law has been made void, rather, in all these points we are to uphold the law in our lives. Mr. Caesar needs to know this. Here is Paul speaking:

"Therefore we conclude that a man is justified by faith without the deeds of the law." Romans 3:28. It is Faith that justifies us, not our works of the law; but does faith and justification do away with the fact that we must do the works of the law? Caesar says **yes,** but here is what Paul says: "Do we then make void the law through faith? God forbid: yea, we establish the law." Romans.3:31. Here we see how plain it is, Faith justifies us, and when we are justified we do not do away with obedience to the law, rather, we actually obey the law! Now whom do we believe? Caesar or Paul? Certainly Paul! Thus all Mr. Caesar's complicated, snake-winding and twisted reasoning cannot destroy the law which is eternal. In the history of antinomianism we are told:

> "Perhaps the most extreme form of anti-nomianism in early Christianity found expression in the Adamite sect in North Africa. The Adamites flourished in the second and third centuries, called the church "Paradise", condemned marriage because Adam had not observed it, and worshipped in the nude. Many Gnostics in the first centuries of the Christian era held the second of these variations of antinomianism-that the Demiurge, not the true God gave the moral law: therefore it should not be kept. Some forms of antinomian Gnosticism survived well into the Middle Ages." **Ibid.,** p.58

These Gnostic sects that were antinomian were first called Nicolaitanes in the Bible before they developed into diverse Gnostical sects with various types of conflicting doctrines. This is what Jesus said about them. "But this thou hast, that thou hatest the deeds of the Nicolaitanes, which I also hate." Revelation 2:6. "So hast thou also them that hold the doctrine of the Nicolaitanes, which thing I hate." Revelation 2:15. We are told that Jesus hates the deeds and doctrine of the Nicolaitanes. What was the doctrine of the Nicolaitanes? History has recorded it, let's look at some examples:

"The Nicolaitanes were a group of professed Christians who believed in a community of wives. When "Thou shall not commit adultery" was quoted, their favourite reply was "We are not under law, but under grace." They claimed they were free from the law and that the Ten Commandments are not binding on Christians."
G. Burnside, **Revelation's Wonders Unfolded**, p.29.

Notice it is the same Evangelicals or Pentecostals teaching of Grace replacing the law, or the law not binding upon the justified Christian that constituted the doctrine of the Nicolaitanes of ancient days which the early apostolic church hated and which God Himself expressly stated that He also hated, yet Evangelicalism is in a large way founded upon that false doctrine. Again we read:

"The Nicolaitanes were persons who excused certain forms of impurity, and made the grace of God a cloak for lasciviousness. I believe the heresy was known in the latter days as Anti-nomianism, which declares that grace is sufficient, and that life is of little moment." G. Campbell Morgan, **The letters of Our Lord**, p.23.

"The Nicolaitanes were the Antinomians of the Asiatic Church. The life and conduct were little thought of and the faith professed was everything. The existence of a sect called Nicolaitanes in the second century is attested by Irenaeus, Tertullian and Clement of Alexander." **The Commentary for Schools**, Edited by C.J. Ellicott, D.D.

"Their doctrines and lives were equally corrupt. They allowed the most abominable lewdness and adulteries, as well as sacrificing of idols: all of which they placed among things indifferent and pleaded for as branches of Christian liberty." John Wesley, **Explanatory Notes Upon The New Testament**, Vol.2.

"Nicolaitanes taught and practiced ritualism without spirituality, knowledge without practice, justification by faith without holiness." Dr. Angus, **The Bible Handbook.**

"The Nicolaitanes used the grace of God as an excuse for the violation of God's law- the moral law." G. Burnside, **Revelation's Wonders Unfolded**, pp.30-31.

In so many ways we can see that Evangelicalism is in fact modern Nicolaitanes, and we must also remember that God hates the "all Grace, no law" doctrine. Observe the further baleful fruits of this teaching in the early history of the church:

"It was this teaching of the Nicolaitanes in the first century that was still corrupting the church of Pergamos a few centuries later, (Rev.2:15) that led to the changing of God's "Royal Law", -the Ten Commandments. The second commandment that forbids the worship of images was dropped from the ten. When the binding nature of that commandment was emphasized, it was lightly brushed aside with "We are not under law, but under grace", "Christians are free from the law", "We enjoy christian liberty." The doctrine of the Nicolaitanes was all too evident." **Ibid.**, p.31.

This antinomianism continued into the Middle Ages, then we are told that it returned in the Protestant reformation while Martin Luther was yet alive.

> *"The two famous antinomian controversies in Christian history occurred in the sixteenth and seventeenth centuries, and involved Martin Luther and Anne Hutchinson, respectively. In fact, it was Luther who actually coined the word "antinomianism" in his theological struggle with his former student, Johann Agricola."* Walter A Elwell, Editor, **Evangelical Dictionary of Theology**, p.58.

> *"This first major theological controversy in Protestant history lasted intermittently from 1537 to 1540. During this time Luther began to stress the role of the law in Christian life and to preach that it was needed to discipline Christians. He also wrote an important theological treatise to refute antinomianism once and for all."* **Against the Antinomians (1539), Ibid.**, p.58

Thus Martin Luther would have rebuked men like Caesar and Johnson and the whole Pentecostal movement had he been alive today. Despite all this he was not perfect in all his teachings. Again, let us read more about this:

> *"Apart from its early appearance in New Testament times, and in Valentinian Gnosticism, the formal rise of Antinomianism has usually been associated with Johannes Agricola, sometimes called*

Islebius, an active leader in the Lutheran Reformation. In his search for some effective principle by which to combat the doctrine of salvation by works, Agricola denied that the believer was in any way obliged to fulfil the moral law. In the Disputation with Luther at Wittenberg (1537), Agricola is alleged to have said that a man was saved by faith alone, without regard to his moral character. These views of Agricola were denounced by Luther as a caricature of the Gospel, but in spite of this, the Antinomians made repeated appeal to Luther's writings and claimed his support for their opinions. This claim, however, is based merely on certain ambiguities in Luther's expressions and general misunderstandings of the Reformer's teachings." Ernest F. Kevan, **The Grace of Law**, p.23.

Thus Evangelical antinomianism is wrong. However, from Germany this cancerous doctrine spread to England, and then to the English colonies on the American continent.

"However, the major controversy over this teaching among Puritans come in New England in the 1630s in connection with an outspoken woman named Anne Marbury Hutchinson, who emigrated to Massachusetts Bay Colony in 1634...At a synod of Congregational churches in 1637 Hutchinson was condemned as an antinomian, enthusiast, and heretic, and banished from the colony. In 1638 she moved to Rhode Island." Walter A. Elwell, Editor, **Evangelical Dictionary of Theology**, pp.58-59.

It was people like this woman and others who spread this cursed antinomianism in America. It came into the Holiness Movement of the late 1800s and thus into the newly emerging Pentecostal movement in the 1900s. Thus, Pentecostalism got its antinomianism not from the Bible as they claim, but from an historical school of antinomianism that moved away from the Lutheran reformation. Anyone who loves truth in Evangelicalism today must acknowledge these things and must make decisions to leave this doomed movement. Paul, the great apostle to the gentiles never condoned ignoring the law for justified or born-again Christians, as far as all his writings are concerned, he upheld the keeping of the law.

Paul says: "Circumcision is nothing, and uncircumcision is nothing, but the keeping of the commandments of God." 1 Corinthians 7:19. In this he laid aside the ceremonial law as nothing and exalted the moral law as the important thing. Certainly this shows that the two laws are not the same, or should not be confused together as Mr. Caesar has done.

Sometimes Evangelicals present love as a replacement or substitute for the Law of Ten Commandments under what they call the New Covenant, but this too is another confusing heresy, nothing in the Bible substantiates this. The facts are that Paul presents the Ten Commandments law **as** love. Love is this law as far as Paul tells us. Look at it in the Bible: "Owe no man anything, but to love one another: for he that loveth another hath fulfilled the law. For this, Thou shalt not commit adultery, Thou shalt not kill, Thou shalt not steal, Thou shalt not bear false witness, Thou shalt not covet: and if there be any other commandment, it is briefly comprehended in this saying, namely, thou shalt love thy neighbour as thyself." Love worketh no ill to his neighbour: therefore love is the fulfilling of the law." Romans 13:8-10. Observe that the Bible says "Love **is** the fulfilling of the law", not Love is the replacement of the law. Also we are told that if there be any other commandment it is briefly comprehended in the saying "Thou shalt love thy neighbour as thyself."

This means that all the other points of the Ten Commandments come under that saying. Having no gods before God, not taking God's name in vain, honouring one's parents, not making or worshipping graven images and keeping the seventh day sabbath holy, all fall under the saying "Thou shalt love thy neighbour as thyself."

If Evangelicals truly believe the Bible and truly love people they will not be anti-nomians for the sake of rejecting the Sabbath, or for any reason whatsoever. The question is: Is it true born-again Christians that hold such anti-nomian teachings? NO! NO! NO!

CHAPTER 8
CULT OR FALSE RELIGION?

The general thesis of this chapter is to prove that the use of the word "cult" in identifying any false religion or any religion for that matter, is not a helpful one, since the description of what constitutes a cult does not prove the religion to be false or not, and by the points that constitute a cult, Jesus and his disciples or the early church could well fit into this description.

The Biblical way is to use "false" or "true" religion, and this would far more help people to judge from the Bible as to what is Truth and who are the bearers of the whole counsel of God.

Funny it is that Evangelicals love to call Seventh-day Adventism a "cult". This is an indication that they are ignorant of their own history. Why do I say this? Because Evangelicalism/Pentecostalism is a new religion that began on January 1st 1901, when one Agnes Ozman began to speak in what we have already discussed as false tongues.

This manifestation of evil spirits in the form of angels of light spread so rapidly in the 20th century that in just a few years before reaching 100 years, and it is already the largest religion in the Christian world apart from the Roman Catholic Church.

Yet this false brand of Christianity started in spiritualism and derives its success from spiritualistic manifestations rather than from the Bible. In an era when it now started, when a little more reasonableness of the human rational was yet in the religious world, this new brand of Christianity with its erratic, over-excited, and unintelligent image was called a "cult".

Here is a little historical point acknowledged by Evangelicals themselves. C. Peter Wagner in the chapter entitled "Characteristics of Pentecostal Church Growth" says:

> *The Pentecostal movement is less than 100 years old, young as such movements go. Only 50 years ago it was still being classified by many along with Jehovah's Witnesses, Mormons, and Christian Science as a false cult."* L. Grant Mc Clung Jr., Editor, **Azusa Street and Beyond**, p. 126.

This is true as the saying goes, now many years later, that they are the "in thing among many Christians", they are not remembered as a "cult", but are now calling Seventh-Day-Adventism by that misleading term. From the experience of facing "...occasional charges of demon possession and mental instability..." Elwell, Editor, **Evangelical Dictionary of Theology**, p. 837.

This new brand of Christianity in now called the great "Third Wave" in Church history. But are they even justified in using the word "cult" to stigmatize any religion whatsoever? The answer is no, because the word serves not to edify anyone as to which is the true church, and as to what is false about false religion. Not only this, but the word "cult" is extremely difficult to use in any sense. Here is what I. Hexham says:

> *"Defining a cult is far more difficult than is often appreciated. Many Evangelicals Christians support the activities of Jews for Jesus and see them as a legitimate missionary group. But members of the Jewish community regard them as an evil and deceptive cult, a fact that well illustrates the problems surrounding the word."* **Ibid.**, p. 289.

In a little booklet, the author Michael Duncan expresses in some ways how difficult it is to use the word "cult" although he applies it and tries to help us identify one. He says:

> *"The word cult really has several meanings...some words have so many unrelated meanings that they should never be used without predefining them. Cult is such a word."* Michael Duncan, **The Christian Advisor Vol. 1, Highly Recommended**, p. 47.

He then attempts to help us understand the word by giving us various meanings such as "Sociological usage (neutral meaning)", "General religious usage (neutral meaning)", "Evangelical Christian usage (negative meaning)", "Fundamentalist Christian usage (negative meaning)", "Popular media usage (very negative meaning)". All this only serves to emphasize the confusion of using the word cult, this is why we would rather use the words "false religion" or "true religion" and derive our definitions from the Bible.

Now how can we explain the origin of the use of the word cult in religion? Mr. Hexham tells us:

> "In its modern form the word "cult" was originally used by Ernst Troeltsch in his classic work, **The Social Teaching of the Christian Churches** (1912), where he classifies religious groups in terms of church, sect, and cult. For Troeltsch the cult represents a mystical or spiritual form of religion that appeals to intellectuals and the educated classes. At the heart of the cult is a spirituality which seeks to enliven a dead orthodoxy. Thus for Troeltsch the early Luther, many Puritans, and pietism can be seen as examples of cultic religion." Walter A. Elwell, Editor, **EvangelicaL Dictionary of Theology**, p. 289.

Thus we see that the first definition of cult was so wrong that its originator's classification confined Luther and many other sincere Christians to a wrong stigmatization.

But Mr. Troeltsch was only the first, he was some years later followed by a Jan van Baalen.

> "More important for the modern usage of the word "cult" has been the development of Evangelical polemics against groups which they have seen as heretical. The classic work on this subject, which probably gave the world its modern usage, is Jan van Baalen's **The**

Chaos of Cults (1938). *In this work van Baalen expounds the beliefs of various religious groups such as theosophy, Christian Science, Mormonism, and Jehovah's Witnesses and subjects them to a rigorous theological critique from an evangelical perspective."* **Ibid.,** p. 289.

One would question why Mr. van Baalen would theologically criticize these false religions and yet call them cult after Mr. Troeltsch, who had a wrong definition. Why did Mr. van Baalen not keep in line with a Biblical definition like "false religion" for example? Nevertheless, Mr. van Baalen's book was the doorway to many Evangelical writers calling religions "cult", and some of them drifted from theological analyses of these religions and began to emphasize things like the morality of those religious leaders and like brainwashing.

"In the last twenty years a large number of evangelical books dealing with cults have appeared. Over the course of time these have increasingly concentrated on the allegedly fraudulent claims of the cults, the immoralities of their leaders, and the ways in which their followers are deceived. As a result, in many cases a transition has occurred from a theological argument refuting the claims of various religious groups to reliance upon psychological arguments which suggest that members of these groups are in some way brainwashed." **Ibid.,** p. 289.

This is the real origin of the use of the word cult with brainwashing and other hard to explain identifying marks. It was the Evangelical's thoughtlessness that caused the word cult to develop along the light it has currently assumed.

But this has not always worked in favor of Evangelicals when they have persisted in calling other religions cults, because they have been maligned by the word being used to identify them.

"This development poses a great danger for evangelical Christianity as can be seen from William Sargent's, **The Battle for the Mind (1957)**. In this book Sargent takes evangelical conversion as a classic example of brainwashing. More recently this argument has been developed by Jim Siegelman and Flo Conway in their popular book **Snapping (1979)**, where the experience of born-again Christians is compared to the process by which people join groups like the Moonies. Such books as these and stories in the media about brainwashing have led to considerable pressure on governments in various American states, Canada, Britain, and Germany for anticonversion laws. These laws are supposedly aimed at groups like the Moonies. But because of their lack of definition (cf. the Lasher Amendment, State of New York in Assembly, 11122-A, March 25, 1980) they are in practice aimed at any form of change of lifestyle brought about by a religious conversion. Today the real problem of cults is the propaganda value of the word "cult" in a secular society." **Ibid.**, p. 289.

Mr. Hexham has himself come to agree that the use of the word cult should discontinue and that it should be replaced with alternative words, plus theological emphasis should be made instead of psychological ones, and all this to save Evangelicals themselves from the stigma of "cult" in a secular society. He says:

> *"Rather than persisting with the use of a word which has now become a propaganda weapon, the academic practice of calling such groups "new religious movements" should be followed. An alternative to this neutral terminology available for Christians who oppose such groups on theological grounds would be to revive the usage of "heretic" or simply call such groups "spiritual counterfeits'. Such a procedure would move the debate away from psychological theories that can be used by secularists against Christianity to the arena of theological discussion and religious argument."* **Ibid.**, p. 289.

This is well said, but we would rather use terms such *as* "true religion" or "false religion" according to the theological argument. Now we shall deal with an example of Evangelical folly in the meaning of the word cult as they have developed it. We are looking at the small booklet produced by Michael Duncan in 1996, and we are examining his article **"Beware of Dangerous Cults".**

> *"...most Evangelicals would define as a cult any Christian religious group which does not accept the historical Christian doctrines (accepting Jesus as Lord and Saviour, Virgin birth, the Trinity etc.). They might consider the Church of Jesus Christ of the Latter Day Saints (the Mormons) as a cult. But they may not (in Trinidad and*

> *Tobago) classify a non-Christian group as a cult. Evangelicals view a cult as a small "bible-toting" group that is in a state of tension with the established **born again** Christian experience."* Michael Duncan, **The Christian Advisor**, Vol. I, Highly Recommended, p. 48.

Here is a classic example of the folly of the use of the word cult. What Mr. Duncan says is true, however you would observe that while the Mormons, the Watchtowers and even Seventh-Day-Adventists are called cults, the Islamic and Hindu religions which really deserve to be called by such a derogatory word, would not qualify. Why? Because they are not "...Christian religious group...", and they are not "...small..." or "bible toting".

Isn't this foolishness? Sure, it is. But a "... small bible-toting group that is in a state of tension with the established born again Christian experience..." would render the early Christian church at its beginning a cult also. So also could be called the Lutheran and Reformed reformations, even early Methodism could fit into that mold as the Pentecostal Movement at its birth and early days. But the folly of the use of the word cult does not end here, because here is how Adventism is viewed by most Evangelicals:

> *'Others might brand any religious group (Christian or otherwise) which deviates from historical Christian belief as a cult."* **Ibid.**, p. 48.

This is true of Adventism which deviates in doctrines like the law, the sabbath, the state of the dead, the judgment etc. But the whole Protestant Movement of the sixteenth century and onwards would also fit into that mold in contrast to Catholicism, because Protestantism emerged from a Christian group who deviated from the historical Christian belief which was Catholic at the time.

However, calling any religion a cult cannot prove its wrongs, but serves only as a propaganda function which closes the mind of the onlooker from being willing to investigate that religion. In his booklet Mr. Duncan gives us "... signs of unhealthy involvement in a cultic group..." **Ibid.**, p. 49. Read the following:

> *"The following signs are intended to be a useful checklist to determine if you, a family member, or a friend have become involved in a destructive Bible based religious cult..."* **Ibid.**, p. 49.

Mr. Duncan plies the psychological method which can be easily turned upon Evangelicals like himself, and none of the points he gives theologically, morally or religiously enlightens anyone, rather they create misjudgment, speculation and distrust if and when placed into practice as a means of identifying a cult. Also bear in mind that one might hold one to four of the points in his mind in a mixed-up way and further compound the problem of identification.

It is evident that anyone who trusts the method given to us by Mr. Duncan has separated themselves from the Holy Spirit of Truth and is without God in this world moving blindly and in darkness. Let's investigate some of his points given to help us identify a dangerous cult. (I have added numbers for easy reference).

1. *'Isolated from all who do not belong to the group and its authority.*

2. *Everyone outside the group is lost; one must be a member.*

3. *Partial commitment or belief is not tolerated.*

4. *Not interested in your type of religious literature.*

5. *Everything outside of the group is satanic, or deceitful.*

6. *Excessive fasting and praying, extreme tension or stress, which may result in eating disorders, chronic depression, acute anxiety, physical exhaustion, or illness.*

7. *Claims that their belief in the group was established through visions or messages claimed to have been given by God. More of a kind of hallucinations.*

8. *Always talking about the group and referrals to dreams, visions or doctrines of its leader.*

9. *Always quoting scriptures accented by the group.*

10. *Refusing to engage in conversation that questions the group beliefs or leaders.*

11. *Almost complete or total domination of the participant's time by the group.*

12. *Attending group activities constantly.*

13. *Loses interest in family, or old friends, or co-workers.*

14. *Will always be witnessing their beliefs to everyone, often in a confrontational or extreme manner:*

15. *Will not allow you to say much during a conversation about group.*

16. *Shows utter disgust or resentment if you refuse to believe the group's doctrines.*

17. *May also deny that there is a heaven or hell. May tell you that heaven or hell is right here or often sets dates for Bible events including the day of Christ's return."* **Ibid.**, p. 49.

So far for these points, a careful reading of the points to identify a cult as presented by Mr. Duncan reveals the stupidity of the psychological method. Many of these points can refer to anyone who is not in any religion whatsoever, or who has joined any religion whether it is Hinduism, Islam, Catholicism or any Evangelical Church or Pentecostal Assembly.

Take point 6 for example, the excessive fasting and praying are done by some Evangelical Churches. What if a person joined one of these churches, and started the excessive fasting and praying, from these points, won't his relatives not think that he is in a cult even though he may have joined a Pentecostal church? Certainly! And the psychological disorders recorded in the same point can emanate from a person's own personal problems even though they may be in a religion.

How is the observer to know that these problems came from the man's personal state and not from a religion? And what if he has those problems while attending, let's say, the church Mr. Duncan personally attends? Does that mean that the person (and obviously Mr. Duncan) are in a cult? By no means.

With regard to point 3, it is well known in the Bible that God Himself tolerates no partial commitment to His cause. He wants us to serve Him with all our being and have our eye single for His glory. Is such a religion that is encouraged by God a cult? Obviously, it is expected, that whatsoever religion a person joins, be it true or false, they must in conscience show the whole-hearted commitment, or why then join the religion at all? Thus that point amounts to nothing with regards to identifying a cult.

Now regarding point 7, when Paul went into new areas that never heard the gospel and sought to establish Christianity, did he not have visions and messages claimed to have been from God? Who could have psychologically examined him to have been hallucinating? None! Then whenever a small church would have been set up, could anyone call them a cult, because Paul established them through visions and messages.

What if the small church now established often referred to Paul's dreams, visions or doctrines with which he founded the church, would they not be a cult also according to point 8? Yes, they would be.

All these brief examples serve to show that it is impossible to use these methods to judge if one is in a false religion or not, they may well serve to turn away from investigating and coming to know the Truth. Nevertheless, inherent in these points are clauses that attack Seventh-Day Adventists from a propaganda stand point, because Evangelicals have failed in theology.

Let us just point out a few more examples of the folly of the use of the word cult and the points used to reveal a cult.

Point 10 is another absurdity, because it may well be a manifestation of a personal fault or bias, and could well be in any religion. A person could be in the real Truth of Jesus Christ, but be failing to abide in that Truth, and through this he could behave that way because of his personal fault or bias. This could also be so for points 15 and 16. Does that mean he is in a **dangerous** cult? By no means at all.

With reference to point 12, everyone expects a new convert to attend group activities constantly since he has much interest. How does that make him belong to a dangerous cult? And who will observe the new convert for twenty-four hours a day for, let's say a month, or maybe two weeks, to learn that there is total domination of the person's time by the group, (how much in the group controls the person? Ten, twenty, thirty?). All these points are totally ridiculous, impractical and are child's play. Thus point 11 is also senseless.

In point 17 the last part reveals the gross ignorance of those who would include date-setting as proof of a cult. Why? Because a reading of Leroy Froom's massive four volumes, **The Prophetic Faith of Our Fathers** would reveal that from the beginning of the church around 50 years after Christ ascended, way down to the late 1800s, the church and all churches have always indulged in date-setting. This would make 1,800 years of the church as it being a cult.

But we could understand Evangelicalism/Pentecostalism holding to such an erroneous point, because they have no real historical connection with those 1800 years of Church history, seeing that they are "Johnny come lately" to the religious scene, only in 1901, and was born not out of scripture, but out of spiritualistic manifestations, and then adopted the whole tottering mass of false doctrines held by the already apostate Holiness Movement of the late 1800s.

One must remember that Evangelicals may make loud noises about "Christ is the Answer" and "ye must be born again", and they may claim to be "Bible believing Christians", but the facts are, much of what they believe is NOT from the Bible, but from tradition attached to the Bible, and they are not careful researchers of the Bible, and when tested, are suddenly revealed to contain mass ignorance of the Bible and history. Thus, it is easy for them to trump up new traditions of men about a cult and palm it off upon members that worship their pastors' words above a simple "Thus said the Lord" from the Bible.

All this talk about cult is absolute nonsense, and must be dismissed for the stupidness that it really is. The closest the Bible comes to the issue of true and false (or vain) religion is this: "If any man among you seem to be religious, and bridleth not his tongue, but deceiveth his own heart, this man's religion is vain. Pure religion and undefiled before God and the Father is this, to visit the fatherless and widows in their affliction, and to keep himself unspotted from the world." James 1:26,27.

There are so many implications in this statement that demolishes Evangelicalism as a false religion. The issue is not cult. Then too, Revelation 14:12 shows us that God's end time church keeps his commandments and has the Faith of Jesus, because, "To the Law and to the testimony: if they speak not according to this word, it is because there is no light in them." Isaiah 8:20.

The people of God in true religion must certainly keep God's Law, and this is the major failure of Evangelicalism. So the issue is whether a religion is true or false in the eyes of God, not fictitious inventions about "cult" that just serve to confuse.

CHAPTER 9

BLOOD-WASHED AND BRAIN-WASHED

The purpose of this chapter is to explain another inaccuracy of the Evangelical's reasoning, dealing with the issue of "blood-washed" and "brain-washed". Most Evangelicals believe that a person who is "blood-washed" is not "brain-washed", but this is wrong. Despite the fact that when Evangelicals use the word "brain-washed" they mean someone who has been subjected to mental depersonalization, and has received a different personality as seen in their behaviour, we shall, however, prove that even the true born-again Christian, whenever he is "blood-washed", he is also certainly "brain-washed."

Here is Mr. Caesar's use of the word "brain-washed".

> "For it must be remembered that most cult members were, at one time, former members of some other Christian denomination, but succumbed to the brainwashing of some cult, simply because they were not grounded in the great truths of the Christian faith." Wordsworth N Caesar, **Blood-washed or Brain-washed, Which?**, p. 54.

Here is the use of the word "brain-washed" in a derogatory sense, yet this can only be so applied to a religion (true or false) if they have learned some old Soviet or espionage technique, something dealing in psychopolitics. Observe this explanation.

> *"The definition of psychopolitics follows. Psychopolitics is the art and science of asserting and maintaining dominion over the thoughts and loyalties of individuals, officers, bureaus, and masses, and the effecting of the conquest of enemy nations through mental healing."* **Brain-Washing, A Synthesis of the Russian Textbook on Psychopolitics**, p. 6.

Yet to achieve what is negatively called "brainwashing" would involve a tremendous amount of funds, officers and property to achieve results.

The process is so complicated and involves so much corruption and iniquity, that just a casual study of the Bible under the Holy Spirit will strongly convince anyone that this is wrong and Satanic and would destroy the movement that is in such practices, so that even the use of secret police or thugs to ensure co-operation would also fail.

Evangelicals like too much fiction, and are often too mentally dull to discern that to claim that someone in a "cult" (false-religion) is brain-washed, is totally stupid, unless by "brain-washed" what is meant is the same method used on a man entering into the Pentecostal religion, or for that matter, any religion.

Observe a little example of how impossible this form of brainwashing is achieved by religions generally.

> "...an overwhelming incidence of neurosis...can be employed as the groundwork for psychopolitical action and a psychopolitical corp." **Ibid.**, p. 7.

> "A simple example of this is the alternation of too low with too high pressures in a chamber, an excellent psychopolitical procedure. The rapidly varied pressure brings about a chaos wherein the individual will cannot act and where other wills then, perforce, assume control" **Ibid.**, p. 14.

> "The technologies of psychopolitics adequately demonstrate the workability of this. Mild shock of the electric variety can, and does, produce the re-cooperation of a rebellious body organ." **Ibid.**, p. 19.

> "As part of this there is the creation of a state of mind in the individual, by actually placing him under duress, and then furnishing him with false evidence to demonstrate that the target of his previous loyalties is, itself, the course of the duress." **Ibid.**, p. 20.

Now the question is, which religion can practice such brainwashing so as to achieve membership and still be functioning as a religion? Seventh day Adventists? No, not so at all. It is the conception of folly and the lack of biblical Faith that causes Evangelicals to believe in this fiction of brainwashing, but it sure serves them well to score propaganda points against Adventism by maligning, vilifying and defaming our characters to scare people from converting to Adventism.

To achieve that kind of brainwashing is virtually impossible unless a religion runs some government espionage agency, and even then, it is still very difficult.

> *"These are the milder methods, but have proven extremely effective. The greatest drawback in their practice is that they require time and concentration, the manufacture of false evidence, and a psychopolitical operator's time."* **Ibid.**, p. 21.

Thus Evangelicals, and people in general, must not be intimidated by shouts of "cult" or "brain-washing" which are mere propaganda terms by dishonest and lying Evangelical preachers to scare people away from investigating the teachings of Adventism and thus stopping them from becoming converted to Adventism.

Now, if by "brain-washing" Evangelicals mean "deceiving" people, they might as well say so, because the Bible warns of "false prophets" using "signs and wonders" to "deceive" if possible "the very elect" (Matthew 24:24), but Evangelicals have already diverted so far from the Bible by using the word "cult" instead of "false religion", that they cannot use "deceive" without going back to the Bible and so nullify the use of the word "cult", thus they prefer to libel God's people with the word "brain-washed"; however, their extremism is proof of their folly and lack of intelligence.

The only other way in which "brain-washed" can be used is in a positive sense which Mr. Caesar apparently doesn't know, because to be "brain-washed" is in reality to be "blood-washed". This is the expressed teaching of the Bible. One cannot be "blood-washed" and not be "brain-washed" for they are like hand in glove.

Yet Mr. Caesar sets the two apart because he believes in the fictional idea of "brain-washed" as we just discussed, or, maybe he does not even understand the real facts.

Read what he says:

> "Now if they are blood-washed their doctrines would surely measure up. However, if they fail to match up, you can be absolutely sure that instead of being blood-washed, they are only brain-washed." Wordsworth N.Caesar, **Blood-washed or Brain-washed, Which?**, p. 56.

Now permit me to enter into the bible to prove that anyone who is "blood-washed" is in fact "brain-washed". Now what does it mean to be brain-washed? It means to have one's values, ideas, and conception of oneself changed so thoroughly that one is a completely **new** person living an altogether new life.

God does this to the born-again person, but not by force or any forcible means. The person must repent of all their old ways of living and their old experiences, and so seek Christ to receive a thoroughly new experience and way of living. Here is how the Bible puts it.

"Therefore if any man be in Christ, he is a new creature: old things are passed away; behold, all things are become new." 2 Corinthians 5:17. **All things** become **new** it says, and "...all things are of God..." 2 Corinthians 5:18. We are carried by Justification or the new birth into an entirely new experience altogether, which constitutes a removal of the norm of things in our existence. It is God "who hath delivered us from the power of darkness, and hath translated us into the kingdom of his dear Son:" Colossians 1:13.

So thoroughly brain-washed are we that, like Paul, we can say "I am crucified with Christ: nevertheless I live; yet not I, but Christ liveth in me: and the life which I now live in the flesh I live by the faith of the Son of God, who loved me, and gave himself for me." Galatians 2:20. But this brain-washing takes place in the mind which is the intellectual powers of the brain. Out of the mind comes forth all sorts of evil. "For from within, out of the heart of men, proceed evil thoughts, adulteries, fornications, murders, thefts, covetousness, wickedness, deceit, lasciviousness, an evil eye, blasphemy, pride, foolishness: All these evil things come from within, and defile the man." Mark 7:21-23.

Because it is also said of man, "...as he thinketh in his heart, so is he..." Proverbs 23:7. David understood the true nature of forgiveness or justification when he said: "Create in me a clean heart, O God; and renew a right spirit within me." Psalm 51:10. Thus Ezekiel could have said God's words: "And I will give them one heart, and I will put a new spirit within you; and I will take away the stony heart out of their flesh, and I will give them an heart of flesh." Ezekiel 11:19.

The word "spirit" in both scriptures is speaking about the experience. A mental experience conscious people always have in their minds or rationalistic powers of the brain. God gives us a new "spirit" or experience as He washes our brains.

Observe Paul's statement: "That ye put off concerning the former conversation (behaviour) the old man (old thoughts), which is corrupt according to the deceitful lusts; and be renewed in the spirit of your mind; and that ye put on the new man (or way of thinking), which after God is created in righteousness and true holiness." Ephesians 4:22-24. If this is not brain-washing, then what is it? So much are we washed that this is what happened to us. "Not by works of righteousness which we have done, but according to his mercy he saved us, by the washing of regeneration, and renewing of the Holy Ghost; which he shed on us abundantly through Jesus Christ our Saviour; that being justified by his grace, we should be made heirs according to the hope of eternal life." Titus 3:5-7.

This washing is a new birth, a spiritual renewal which constitutes our justification. We are really brain-washed because our every thought is dominated by Christ. "Casting down imaginations, and every high thing that exalteth itself against the knowledge of God, and bringing into captivity every thought to the obedience of Christ;" 2 Corinthians 10:5. We are made into a completely different person. "And the Spirit of the LORD will come upon thee, and thou shalt prophesy with them, and shalt be turned into another man." 1 Samuel. 10:6. Why was it so with Saul at first? Because "...God gave him another heart..." 1 Samuel 10:9. Thus we have clearly seen that true Christians are really brain-washed.

Now what does "blood-washed" mean? First we must understand that by the blood of Christ, His death is not meant, neither is it His literal blood. His blood is used as a symbol for life which Christ came to give. "For the life of the flesh is in the blood: and I have given to you upon the altar to make an atonement for your souls: for it is the blood that maketh an atonement for the soul." Leviticus 17:11. "For it is the life of all flesh; the blood of it is for the life thereof: therefore I said unto the children of Israel, ye shall eat the blood of no manner of flesh; for the life of all flesh is the blood thereof:..." Leviticus 17:14. "Only be sure that thou eat not the blood: for the blood is the life; and thou mayest not eat the life with the flesh." Deuteronomy 12:23.

Here is unmistakable evidence that blood means "life". But what is life? "And this is life eternal, that they might know thee the only true God, and Jesus Christ, whom thou hast sent." John 17:3. Life according to the Bible is a knowledge of God and Christ, this is holy, spiritual knowledge revealed by the Spirit. This knowledge is the word of Truth which washes us. "That he might sanctify and cleanse it with the washing of water by the word," Ephesians 5:26. So to be blood-washed is to be life washed, or to be washed by the knowledge of God and Christ. This is also explained as the light or knowledge washing away the darkness of sin from in our hearts. "For God, who commanded the light to shine out of darkness, hath shined in our hearts, to give the light of the knowledge of the glory of God in the face of Jesus Christ." 2 Corinthians 4:6.

It is also presented as the new birth by the word of God. "Of his own will begat he us with the word of truth, that we should be a kind of first fruits of his creatures." James 1:18. "Being born again, not of corruptible seed, but of incorruptible, by the word of God, which liveth and abideth for ever." 1 Peter 1:23.

It is also presented as: "...Except a man be born of water and of the Spirit, he cannot enter into the kingdom of God." John 3:5. The "...Spirit is truth." 1 John 5:6. So to be born of the Spirit is to be born of the word of truth or the knowledge of God and Christ which is called "Life" in John 17:3.

To be blood-washed then, is to be brain-washed, it is the same as saying that the word of truth or the word of life (John 6:63) washes or purifies our minds from the old way of thinking or the old mental values that are sinful, and this changes our way of living or our behaviour.

This concept is presented in the Psalm. "Wherewithal shall a young man cleanse his way? By taking heed thereto according to thy word." "Thy word have I hid in mine heart, that I might not sin against thee." Psalm 119:9,11.

Ezekiel also tells us in another way that "blood-washing" (washing by the word of life) is "brain-washing" (being given a new mind and experience). "Then will I sprinkle clean water upon you, and ye shall be clean: from all your filthiness, and from all your idols, will I cleanse you. A new heart also will I give you, and a new spirit will I put within you: and I will take away the stony heart out of your flesh and I will give you an heart of flesh. And I will put my spirit within you, and cause you to walk in my statutes, and ye shall keep my judgments, and do them." Ezekiel 36:25-27.

With a new experience and a new way of thinking, we cannot only "...prove what is that good, and acceptable, and perfect, will of God." Romans 12:2, but we can also "...keep his commandments, and do those things that are pleasing in his sight." 1 John 3:22.

Evangelicals do not like to keep or even emphasize keeping God's Law, so they have no moral evidence of being blood-washed, yet the Bible tells us that "... faith, if it hath not works, is dead, being alone." James 2:17.

So in conclusion of this topic, we can truly say that to be "blood-washed" is to be "brain-washed". One who is washed in the Life of Christ or washed in the "knowledge of God and Jesus Christ" (John 17:3), undergoes a mental washing, a moral or spiritual washing, and that is the removal of the old values of the carnal mind from the present consciousness as the ideal. This is substituted with the divine thought or mind of faith and righteousness (God's nature) which motivates and empowers us to walk in obedience to the works of the Law of the Ten Commandments.

This is but a part of the great mystery of salvation or the Plan of Salvation which alone can save us. If Mr. Caesar and any Evangelical do not know this Plan they cannot be saved, it's as plain as that, and all one has to do is to read the twisted and warped materials written by this man to confirm what is said.

Finally, of the redeemed saints we are told. "...These are they which...have washed their robes, and made them white in the blood of the Lamb." Revelation 7:14, and "...the fine linen is the righteousness of saints." Revelation 19:8. We must undergo a change from sin to righteousness, from corruption to purity, it's the only thing God can do to save us, it's the **only way** of salvation. Thus Evangelicals must truly repent so that they can be blood-washed and brain-washed by the Holy Spirit.

CONCLUSION

What then do we think about Evangelicalism/Pentecostalism? The sum total of my research, which is limited because of the scarcity of original materials on this topic, has afforded me to clearly see that this is a modern rebirth of spiritualism, in a Christian cultural image.

I believe that Satan and his evil angels had Evangelicalism as their type of delusionary religion for the end time, and as they thought that the end would come around the time of the Judgement in 1844 or sometime shortly after, they brought up this type of so-called Christian-spiritualism in the 1830's. Firstly, to destroy many people; but as the end did not come and as the spiritual rationalistic sensibilities of people were too moral to accept this type of emotional religion, it largely died down but arose again in the 1900's, during the last century before the second coming of Christ.

The theological climate of the declining Holiness churches produced a perfect environment for the re-emergence of this Christian spiritualism, so that by 1901 Satan moved upon Miss Agnes Ozman and so began the modern Evangelical Movement that gained its greatest impetus in the Azusa Street Movement of 1906-1909.

One of the best ways to access the Evangelical/Pentecostal Movement is to briefly investigate its prototype in the Irvingite Movement of the 1830's. Here one receives a remarkable account of the same climate, morality and typology of the Pentecostal spirit, but one can see in all this, clear evidence that Irvingism was wrong just as Evangelicalism today is wrong.

The whole thing is nothing but a revival of spiritualism wearing a Christian form. As such, members are called to come out of this Babylonian false religion into the Truth of God's Word.

Of Mr. Irving we are told:

> "Edward Irving was a Presbyterian minister who served in London from 1822 until his death in 1834. But he could also be termed a Pentecostal. That is, during his last five years his doctrinal position was virtually that of the Pentecostal body of today. He believed God was then granting a restoration of the apostolic gifts, especially those of tongues, healing, and prophecy. Although he preceded our day by a century and a half, he well deserves the recognition he has recently begun to receive as forerunner of the Charismatic Movement." Arnold Dallimore, **Forerunner of the Charismatic Movement**, p. 7.

As we have read earlier in this book, the basic teaching of Evangelicalism is that "tongues speaking" is the real evidence of the reception of the Holy Spirit, thus proof that their movement is of God.

164

It began with this so-called "tongues speaking", spread by "tongues speaking" and is based primarily on "tongues speaking". Thus we must investigate "tongues speaking" as it broke out in Mr. Irving's time.

"But above all, both Mary and this company around her had one supreme expectation in mind - she was to be the first to experience the renewed outpouring of the charismatic gifts - she was to receive "the gift of tongues",...On a Sunday evening in the month of March (1830), Mary, in the presence of a few friends, began to utter sounds to them incomprehensible, and believed by her to be a tongue such as of old might have been spoken on the day of Pentecost, or among the Christians of Corinth. This was of course, a historic event. It was the first experience of "speaking in tongues" in the Irvingite movement. Moreover, Mary was sure she was not merely uttering incomprehensible sounds. She was certain she was speaking a language. She asserted it was the language of a people on a remote island in the South Seas-the Pelew Islanders, a people of whom she had been reading. And to this gift she shortly added another: that of automatic writing. At times she would pass into a kind of trancelike condition in which she would seize a pencil and with amazing speed fill pages of paper with script. The characters she used were not those of the English or any other known language, and therefore the whole experience was believed to be miraculous and the writing was said to be in a foreign tongue. Of course, news of Mary Campbell's "gift of tongues" spread rapidly." **Ibid.,** pp. 120, 121.

A quick look at what is recorded above should convince everyone that this occurrence has no Biblical parallel. This phenomenon serves nothing but to prove that "God" miraculously used Mary Campbell. There was no edification, no teaching even from the so-called unknown script she wrote, but we see in this a parallel to the outbreak of "tongues speaking" as occurred under Charles Parham in 1901. It was a woman who first babbled, and she also wrote in a language miraculously at that time, she claimed it was Chinese language, but it was proven to be no such thing but a fraud. So much for Agnes Ozman.

Let's look back to 1830.

> "Margaret Mc Donald was also a semi-invalid. Early in 1830 she had an experience in which she received, she said, "the gift of prophecy." And a little later (three weeks after Mary Campbell's "tongues" experience) the two Mc Donald brothers had a similar experience and each "spoke in tongues'. The minister at Row, Mc Leod Campbell's learning of these events, paid a visit to the Mc Donald home that he might see and hear for himself. He hoped the tongues were of divine origin, but in order to test them he said they ought to be interpreted. Thereupon James broke out into incomprehensible sounds and George gave an interpretation." Behold He cometh-Jesus cometh." **Ibid.,** p. 122.

Certainly, you must have seen the folly in this whole thing. This child Margaret Mc Donald is the only one from whom the "rapture" theory came. Nobody nor church of the Christian faith ever taught it before her, yet her so-called "gift of prophecy" and "tongues speaking" gave birth to this damnable heresy; it certainly was not a Bible doctrine, it came from spiritualistic manifestations which emanated from the great deceiver, Satan himself. You can see this again in the following behavior.

> "Following her experience, Mary and her friends continued to meet upstairs in the Campbell home as usual, praying especially that all of them might receive the gift of tongues and thus be equipped to begin their missionary careers. But in the room beneath there still lay Mary's brother Samuel, and he was now near to death. Moreover, he was 'racked through his whole frame by the shouting and leaping and singing overhead." Yet despite his condition 'he rallied...his decaying energies, left his pillow and ascended the stairs...entered the room and entreated them to be quiet." But, like Pastor Story, the dying was told (not by Mary but by some of the others), "Get thee behind me, Satan!" And in a few days' time he was dead." **Ibid.**, p. 123.

No comment is needed on the above statement, readers can see that the whole undertaking was not of God. However, read another quotation which shows that "tongues speaking" was not of God:

> "The gift of tongues did not come as a direct action from heaven, but means were usually employed to bring it about. Miss Cardale was considered especially proficient in this regard, and made it her practice to say to a seeker, 'Yield your tongue, yield your tongue,

yield your tongue to the Holy Ghost!" Likewise, Mary Caird, with her mystical but forceful personality, did much instructing as to how to speak in tongues and was exceptionally successful in the task." **Ibid.,** p. 134.

Of course no such thing happened in the apostolic period, such help to speak in tongues need not be since the living Holy Spirit gives this as a gift when needed to advance God's work.

We can now look at some of the words of this so-called "tongues speaking", and it shall be observed that it has the hallmarks of Satan as a gross falsehood. Here are some words spoken as tongues. We have: "gthis dil emma sumo", "Hozequinalta stare, Hozehamenan-ostra", "Casa sera hasta caro", "yeo cogo nomo", and "Holimoth holif awthaw", (**Ibid.**, 138). What can we make of this nonsense? Is this gibberish genuine tongues? Not at all. It is not even a language; and to add more...

'There were also eyewitness accounts that contained such statements as: 'the terrible Crash (cras- cras- era-Crash!!!) with which the utterance began", 'a violent exertion of the muscles at the back of the jaw bone"; 'She screamed until, from exhaustion her voice gradually died away"; 'Suddenly an appalling shriek seemed to rend the roof, which was repeated with heart-chilling effect...and then suddenly a torrent of unintelligible words. The young lady was quite scarlet." **Ibid.,** pp. 140-141.

"...going next evening to call on Irving, we found the house all decked out for this same 'speaking with tongues", and as we talked a moment with Irving who had come down to us, there rose a shriek in the upper story of the house, statement and presently he exclaimed, "There is one prophesying, come up and hear her!" We hesitated to go, but he forced us up into a back room and we could hear the wretched creature raving like one possessed, hooing and haaing and talking as insensibly as one would do with a pint of brandy in his stomach, till after some ten minutes she seemed to grow tired and become silent. Nothing so shocking and unspeakably deplorable was it ever my lot to hear." **Ibid.,** p.141.

"But while Miss Hall was in the vestry another woman was moved to utterance and rising from her seat she ran down the side aisle and out of the Church through the principle door...The sudden, doleful and unintelligible sounds, being heard by all the congregation (about 1500 or 2000 persons), produced the utmost confusion..." **Ibid.,** p. 142.

Much more can be documented to expose the folly of this kind of Christianity, however, it was too controversial and too much below the moral sensibilities of the people at that time and the church eventually deteriorated setting up a system of apostles and prophets (as Pentecostalism/Evangelicalism today), but it then dwindled and many members of the church that Irving set up joined the Roman Catholic Church. Thus we see that Satan's experiment to set up his last day form of "Christian" spiritualism was a bit too premature and it eventually failed yet to be revived in the 1900's.

Now, we are many years into this spiritualism to the effect that it is accepted by the public as genuine Christianity, but a closer look at it in the light of pure Bible doctrine will expose it for what it is, and this is what I have done in this book.

However, there are quite a number of homepages being put out on the Internet about the "tongue speaking" of many Evangelical leaders, so that those who have computers can tap into these pages and receive information on this "tongue" phenomenon which is indeed Satanic.

The "tongues" spoken by some leaders have been closely investigated with the speaking being slowed down only to reveal English words placed, spaced out in sentences. These words often blaspheme, praise Satan, or use obscene phrases. Yes, this is what "tongue speaking" among Evangelicals/Pentecostals is all about.

I have abundant proof about these facts, some of which I will present that it may be clearly seen that this anti-nomian religion is indeed Satanic spiritualism.

Many have heard of Mr. Kenneth Copeland, here are some of the points about him revealed on some homepages:

"Kenneth Copeland while pretending to be speaking in tongues says the words, "Come take the mark of the Beast" as he invites Dennis Bourke to come forward for ministry...

Kenneth Copeland says the words, "Tell my brother now take the beast, take together Satan here, yeah have the mark off from the beast" as he communicates with Rodney Howard Browne in supposed tongues...

Kenneth Copeland says the words, "I bun you Satan our lord tie the money" as a man is doing a sort of running dance...

Kenneth Copeland says the words, "Yes, yes, yes forwards I'ma ina im, im in sins" and then he has a good laugh.

Kenneth Copeland begins speaking in what is supposed to be tongues by saying the words "Yeah I like my devil".

Kenneth Copeland waving his left hand and disgustingly doing the sign of allegiance to Satan while at the same time saying the words, "Yeah I'm a demon'.

Kenneth Copeland speaking in his supposed tongues language says the words, "Ab...hole monendo I got a demon." Kenneth Copeland while trying to pronounce the word "faithful" says the 'F' word, he says, "f, fa, f..k" and then quickly begins to speak in tongues to cover up what he said by making out that it was all tongues." **The Toronto Blessing Unmasked**, pp. 1,2.

Did you read that? This pastor cursed using obscene language and then sought to cover it up by using tongues to fool people. The homepages we are quoting from even reveal that Mr. Copeland is a 33rd Degree Freemason.

What does all this show? That Evangelicalism/Pentecostalism is Satanic spiritualism. Again let me quote some more from the same document:

"A demon speaks out of a lady that Rodney Howard Browne ministers to, says the words, "More Satan master" as the lady is manifesting the laughter and demonic tongues.

A Satanist who is posing as a Christian pastor while he is following Rodney Howard Browne puts his hand on a lady to minister to her and says the words, "She ta soro Satan I'm gonna talk for you"

Mike Evans says the words, "Take over Satan" when he is being ministered to by Kenneth Copeland and Rodney Howard Browne.

Female demonic voice and Dennis Bourke combine to say, "Our Satan's here (female voice), "Yes he is" (Dennis Bourke) while Dennis Bourke is manifesting. A demon speaks out of someone in the audience who is experiencing the movement and says the words, "More our devil" or "More our Satan" just before Rick Shelton is about to get struck by a spirit that causes him to lose his memory and behave weirdly.

While under the influence of the spirit that is causing him to experience loss of memory, behave weirdly, Rick Shelton can be heard saying the words, "I worship Satan."

Mike Evans can be heard saying the words, "Yes our Satan master" faintly in the background as he raised his right hand in the air in worship of the presence that is moving in the meeting.

Jesse Duplantis says the words, "Take over my Satan you're moving here Satan" when pretending to be speaking in tongues.

Jesse Duplantis again communicates with Satan when pretending to be speaking in tongues, this time he can be heard saying "More our Satan thank you lord."

Jesse Duplantis quickly says the words, 'Glory be to Satan who's on me, thank you lord" when Kenneth Copeland tells him to turn his throat loose in Jesus' name." **Ibid.**, pp. 1-7.

Do you really think all this is of God? Was apostolic religion and worship anything like the Satanic riot we see transpiring as worship to God? Where do we find Jesus Christ teaching such religious practices? Yet all this passes in the name of God in Evangelicalism/Pentecostalism.

Let us again look at some obscene language coming from Mr. Copeland as tongues speaking:

"Kenneth Copeland disgustingly says the words, 'F..k your mother, the devil's in me, yes" while pretending to be speaking in tongues, and then begins to prophesy over Rodney Browne.

As Rodney Howard Browne is ministering the laughter Kenneth Copeland makes a statement that shows that these men worship Bacchus, the god of wine. He says the words, "Don't f..k me don't take our Bacchus."

Kenneth Copeland says the words, "Tell the damn mike yes I'm a devil in us" as Rodney Howard Browne puts the microphone on the mouth of a lady who is experiencing the laughter." **Ibid.**, pp. 1-7.

There is much, much more on this homepage that exposes the Satanism of Evangelicalism/Pentecostalism. We have men who are supposed to be Christians praising the devil in their "tongues" saying words and phrases like:

"Socoro devil socori ba ba ba ba in un "el pus", "Bonshkoste ba ba bug our devil". "There goes our ba ba there Satan under", 'Bind him, I hear thee, my boy, my Satan's in me", "Busundra my Satan", 'Naughty pa rule my Satan, naughty master", "Warst our Satan master", "Our devil beast", 'B. stard master Satan help me I'm a demon", "Olival I'm evil, ardos daughter Satan I love her', 'Do whatever you want Satan's in us", "I worship Satan," "She ta soro Satan I'm gonna talk for you", "Might be move Satan, might be move Satan, might be move Satan's here", "Our Satan you are talking master", "Satan master dine", "All hail Satan yes", "My girl

Satan", "You will move Satan", "Horapasia Satan", "I said I love the devil, la, la, la, la ...", "Come work our Satan nasty", and many many more evil phrases."

All this serves to highlight that this religious phenomenon of the 1830's which returned much more in the 1900's was and is of the devil. It is not true Christianity. It is spiritualism; thus, this religion must be abandoned and Thusia Seventh-Day Adventist must be joined by accepting the end time developed Faith of Christ.

Just imagine this statement coming from Kenneth Copeland. He says:

"You don't have a God in you. You are one!" **Ibid.**, p. 6.

Is this not the spiritualistic lie of the voice of Satan when he said to Eve: "...ye shall be as gods..." (Genesis 3:5)? Yes it is, and even the famous Benny Hinn is found to be in the same spiritualism and Satan worship. He is heard chanting the words:

"Demon demon demon demon, release im release im release im, release im, release im." **Benny Hinn.**, p. 2.

All these facts can be found on the Internet so anyone can check it for oneself. Just check **Cult Busters** on geocitees.com for this information. Plus, one can get other links on Mr. Copeland such as:

http://www.iclnet.org/pub/resources/text/cri/cri-jrnl/crjoll9a.txt

(first retrieved in November, 1997), or

http://www.rapidnet.com/jbeard/bdm/exposes/copeland/general.htm (first retrieved in November, 1997)

There are more sites, but they are all very sobering. They all bring us to the exact thing which God has said. "For such are false apostles, deceitful workers, transforming themselves into the apostles of Christ. And no marvel; for Satan himself is transformed into an angel of light. Therefore it is no great thing if his ministers also be transformed as the ministers of righteousness; whose end shall be according to their works."2 Corinthians 11:13-15.

Evangelicalism/Pentecostalism is the epitome of apostasy of the last days. It is rank spiritualism converted over to the forms of Christianity, and Satan can work so many miracles for them because he knows that ninety-nine percent of their doctrines are erroneous and devilish, and to confirm them by signs and wonders will cause people to embrace them preparatory for being lost in utter darkness.

In plain speaking, the best thing anyone can do for Evangelicalism/Pentecostalism is to abandon it all together. Both members and ministers should evacuate that spiritualistic religion urgently, in the hope of recovery from a mind of confusion. The errors of this sect in Christianity are multiplying like sardines and they are falling lower and lower down the scale of mental rationalism. People's minds and emotions are becoming damaged, and a fanatical and extremist instability has taken hold of the people.

The people of this religion are unable to reason properly to be able to see Bible truth. They do not have much appetite for holiness and their hypocrisy and insincerity have increased tenfold. They are plain worldlings but just taking the name of Christ. The worst iniquity both in secret and in public exists. Truth having taken flight, has left darkness alone, and this religion was born in error and spiritualism, thus although it carries the name Christian, it is yet merely the ancient pagan spiritualism disguised as Christianity.

People must "come out of her" (Revelation 18:6) lest they partake of the retribution soon to come. It is only Faith, the Faith of Jesus Christ which justifies us or gives to us Righteousness (Galatians 2:16; Philippians 3:9), that we must receive so that we shall be just and live by Faith (Romans 1:17).

Evangelicalism/Pentecostalism needs this Faith of Jesus Christ which contains Righteousness, they are not yet righteous by Faith, they have only works-Righteousness, and this cannot avail in the judgment. Except one has the Faith of Jesus Christ which gives spiritual Righteousness, the Divine Nature, into the person (Romans 3:21,22) and this Faith also calls us to do the works of the Law (Romans 3:21), so that God in us (Galatians 2:20) could work all our works in us (Isaiah 26:12), the religion is baptized Spiritualism and that is all.

We call upon people to "Come out of Babylon", before it is too late. Repent ye and receive the gospel, the only hope of global salvation. Thus you shall have the blessed hope looking for the coming of Christ.

May God bless all readers to the point of enlightenment and true and genuine change for the better. Amen and Amen.

APPENDIX

1. The Evangelicals emphasize "freedom from condemnation" which they call justification, as the Gospel of Salvation. Read what some of them have to say.

> a. *"Looking at salvation more closely, the Bible describes those who trust in Christ as 'saved', 'being saved' and 'shall be saved'. "We are saved from the penalty, or consequences, of sin which is a disintegrating and deadening effect on our spirits making us unresponsive to God and his love. The consequences and judgment of sins are removed by Christ's work and we are made alive to God."* Roger Forster, **Saving Faith**, p. 7.

"How could Luther be put right with God when he was confronted by God's righteousness? If God was righteous and just, Luther knew himself condemned...As light dawned in his soul he saw that the justice of God would not condemn him but would, if he had faith, release him into the freedom of a child of God (see Romans 8:21). God had made a way through the death of his son Jesus that would enable God himself to remain righteous and yet make Luther, and anyone who wanted to believe, right with him also. To be justified

179

is to be made right with God, or righteous. (The two words are the same in Greek)...Because of Jesus Christ's voluntary death on our behalf, God forgives us and puts us right with him...So the Bible says we shall not come into judgment, but are passed from death to life. God's fire of anger at sin has passed over us, scorching Christ and freeing us. Romans 5:9 says, 'By his death we are now put right with God; how much more, then, will we be saved by him from God's anger! (GNB).

"It is only as we are sure that the death of the Lord Jesus Christ has provided a safe ground for us to stand before God that we have the confidence to enter by faith through the power of the Holy Spirit into the saving life of Christ. The good news of salvation is to remove this uncertainty so that we feel secure in God. Assured of our acceptance by God through Christ's death for our sins, any man or woman may enter into a whole new sphere of existence where there is deliverance from fears and Satan...Nothing could shift this sense of self-loathing and rejection by God until he was told, and he accepted, that when Jesus was on the cross he was made equally offensive." **Ibid.**, pp. 10-13.

"As we declare the blood of Christ, the accuser has no grip of guilt on his victim for Christ's death has removed everything God had against him and the blood of Jesus purifies from all sin." **Ibid.**, p. 24.

b. "The Gospel inherently contains a stigma. There's nothing more offensive than the blood, which Jesus shed when He died on the cross. There is no greater offence than the premise that a person is actually saved from the wrath of God by simple trust in the blood of Jesus, and the devil will do anything to get us away from that." R. T. Kendall, **He Saves**, p. 14.

"We will see the 'Gospel- plus' in many quarters...which is always the result of attempting to destigmatize the Gospel. At the other extreme there are still those who say, 'Yes, we believe in justification by faith, but it is given upon the condition of obedience to the Law.' There you are, right back to the very thing Paul had to correct in the early church. It always cuts the very jugular vein of the Gospel.

"One difficulty with the view that you are saved upon condition of good behavior is that you will never have assurance that you are saved. Who among us will ever feel holy enough to be able to say, 'Yes, I now believe I'm saved'? That is inviting self-righteousness in its most blatant form." **Ibid.**, p. 16.

"This generation knows almost nothing about the wrath of God. Why did Jesus die on the cross? Was there no other way we could be saved? Why wasn't it by the Sermon on the Mount, which He taught? Or the ethic of loving your enemy, and doing good to those who mistreat you? Why did He have to die? It is because of sin and God had to deal with sin...But God hates these things so much that

the only way He could forgive them is by sending His Son into the world to die on a cross. The next time you are ready to do something that you know is wrong, remember what it cost God to save men.

When a person is saved it is as though it were a silent thing. That is to say it happens in the heart." **Ibid.**, p. 20.

"You may be a moral person, and I would not want you to be any other kind of person. But if you are trusting that morality for your salvation, you are just as lost as the most immoral person walking the streets of London or New York. You have got to give up any hope that your morality will save you, and come instead to the place where you see you have got no bargaining power. That is, with God." **Ibid.**, p. 22.

"Can God be just and merciful at the same time? The answer is yes: He sent His Son into the world and punished Him – the God – man who never sinned – for our sins. The prophet Isaiah wrote, 'The Lord hath laid on him (Jesus) the iniquity of us all' (Isa. 53:6). He who knew no sin was 'made sin' (2 Cor. 5:21), thus satisfying God's justice so that He could be merciful to us. This is the heart of the Gospel: God punished Jesus for what we did." **Ibid.**, p. 26.

"When Jesus fulfilled the law He did so by keeping it all...Jesus was our substitute, then, not only by His death on the cross but by His life...In a word: Jesus believed for us; He obeyed for us. When He was crucified God's wrath was actively executed upon Jesus our substitute...By substitution it means Jesus took our place. By

satisfaction it means that God's justice was satisfied by what Jesus did." **Ibid.**, p. 28.

c. *"It was finished for every single one of us 2,000 years ago on that cross. Our sins were all forgiven clear back there, 2,000 years ago. The righteous life was completely lived and completely given for you and me 2,000 years ago. It's done! It is finished! Christ was taken down off that cross and our sins were taken down with Him. He was buried in the tomb. And your sins and my sins were buried there, too!"* Steve Marshall, **What's the Difference?**, p. 16.

"What we've just talked about is **justification.** *Justification is what Christ did* **for** *us in His life and His death. All right? Justification is God's accepting you just as if you yourself had done what Jesus did. You didn't do it, your substitute did it. But God accepts you because of what your substitute did for you. It's a finished work. Justification, the gospel, is a finished work. All right? It's done. 2,000 years ago. Settled. Your sins were forgiven. You were given the gift of eternal life and Christ's righteousness. His obedient life. Justification, what Jesus did in His life and His death, is the* **cause** *of our salvation. The cause. That's what saves us."* **Ibid.**, p. 19.

"There are two terms that go along with justification and sanctification. One is **imputed righteousness,** *and the other is* **imparted righteousness.** *Imputed righteousness has to do with*

justification. What does "imputed" mean? What is the middle of the word? **Put.** *Impute means to put something to someone's credit or account. So,* **imputed righteousness** *is Christ's righteousness, His 100% perfect, obedient, life that is* **put** *to your credit, when you accept Him as your Saviour. God looks at your spiritual bank account before you accept Christ, and it's empty. You accept the Lord Jesus Christ, and instantly it's full. God the Father* **puts** *Christ's perfect, 100% righteous life to your credit. He fills your spiritual bank account to overflowing with perfect righteousness. Christ's own righteousness is imputed to you. It's put to your account. Imparted righteousness is righteousness that becomes a* **part** *of you. It's the same as sanctification. It's becoming like Christ. But it* **does not save you.** *The imputed righteousness saves you. The imparted righteousness* **changes** *you."* **Ibid.**, p. 20.

"When you and I accept the Lord Jesus Christ as our Saviour, we ourselves are guilty, wretched sinners. But the moment we accept Him as our Saviour, God imputes to us Christ's perfect righteousness. He puts to our account that perfect, righteous, obedient life. In ourselves, we're still sinners. But God doesn't look at us in ourselves. He looks at us in the robe of Christ's righteousness. He looks at us with Christ's righteousness imputed to us. And how does He judge us now? **Not guilty!** *Innocent! And that's what imputed righteousness means. Though we are still sinners, we still fail, we may fall. But God doesn't see that. As we trust in Jesus, He sees Christ's perfect obedience in place of our*

imperfect obedience...Justification is the finished work of the Lord Jesus Christ for us 2,000 years ago. It's done. We accept it. And immediately as we accept it, sanctification begins in our lives and we begin to be changed." **Ibid.**, p. 21.

"Justification does not just take care of your past sin. You need justification, the work of Jesus Christ, to cover your good deeds, too! You need it to make your sanctification acceptable to God. Even your obedience by the power of the Holy Spirit is not acceptable to God, unless it is covered by the perfect righteousness of Jesus Christ. You can never come to the place where you don't need Jesus. You need the righteousness of Jesus (justification) to cover even your sanctification life." **Ibid.**, p. 23.

*"Our religious services—all of the good things we do because of our love for God—are so polluted by self that they can't be acceptable to God unless the merit and blood of Jesus Christ covers them. Justification is like an umbrella, covering both our sins and our good works. The things we do are never acceptable unless covered by what Jesus did. They can never, by themselves, be of value with God...The merit and blood of Jesus Christ is the only thing that makes our good works, our prayers, our requests and our praise acceptable to God...***Sanctification*** has to be ***saturated*** in the ***justification***—the blood of Jesus—before it can be accepted by God...The gospel is that perfect work of God, accepting us as if we had done it, when we didn't do it at all, but Christ Jesus did it. That's the gospel. Isn't that fantastic?"* **Ibid.**, p. 25.

"And this is what He gave me. Justification is the **ground** *of our salvation. It's the ground. Who did it? Jesus did it. Justification is the gospel. Jesus' life and Jesus' death, that which He did for us 2,000 years ago. It's finished. It's all done...We'll never be blown away by false winds of doctrine if we have hold of the ground—the finished work of Jesus Christ—the gospel...As a Christian has a firm hold on the finished work of Jesus Christ, and meditates on the finished work of Jesus Christ, he begins to be changed."* **Ibid.**, p. 26.

"Whom the Lord justifies, He always sanctifies. The two always go together. One saves. The other changes. One is the cause. The other is the effect. Sanctification does not save you. And it does not add anything to your salvation except proof—visible proof—to the world that you've accepted the Lord Jesus Christ as your Saviour. That's what it's all about." **Ibid.**, pp. 28-29.

"The teacher takes the belt. "Crack!" goes the belt. "Crack!" again and again. Welts rise up on John's back. Five, six. Blood spurts. Seven, eight, nine, 10,11. Mr. Primble has to look away. Twelve, 13, 14, 15. And it is finished. John, all lacerated and bleeding, straightens up. Blood is running down his back. Now little Timmy turns around and as he sees the blood, tears stream down his face. He throws his arms around John and he hugs John and he says, "Oh, John—I'll love you forever!"

"That's the gospel, saved by our substitute meeting the demands of the law for us. And the result of the gospel is a heart broken in love.

A heart that will love God and all the souls He died for, forever. So, you see, there is a difference between justification and sanctification. Justification saves us. Sanctification changes us. Justification is our ticket to eternal life. Sanctification is the proof that we have accepted the ticket and are on board. But always remember that your peace with God and your assurance of eternal life is in what Jesus did for you, not what you do for Him." **Ibid.,** pp. 37-38.

2. What does God require of us? Does He require freedom from the fact that we are condemned? Or is it holiness of character? Deuteronomy 10:12,13; Micah 6:8.

3. Man's problem is the lawlessness of his carnal mind. Romans 8:7.

4. He needs a new, pure, changed heart. Psalm 51:10; Romans 12:2.

5. A heart to love God and obey His Law. Deuteronomy 30:6,10-16.

6. This Law is holy. Romans 7:12.

7. Thus in keeping it by Faith man is made holy. James 2:20; Deuteronomy 28:9.

8. God emphasizes holy living, not deliverance from condemnation. Leviticus 19:2; Leviticus 20:26.

9. It is **after** we have a holy life that we shall escape condemnation. Romans 8:4,1.

10. What were the words emphasized on the High Priest's helmet? "Holiness unto the Lord!". Exodus 28:36; Exodus 39:30,31.

11. It is this "holiness" that makes us acceptable unto the Lord, not freedom from penalty. Exodus 28:36-38.

12. What was the import of this "Holiness to the Lord" upon the priest's helmet?

> "What have we written on our forehead? The High Priest bore the inscription **HOLINESS TO THE LORD**. This is the crowning fact, the culmination of everything. Without this "all else is worthless – Forms, ceremonies, priestly attire, sacrifice, prayer, are mockeries. It required primarily the high priest himself to be holy; but it was a call to the whole nation, whose representative the high priest was, that they should be "a holy nation", "a kingdom of priests", and should consecrate themselves heart and soul to Jehovah". To have **HOLINESS TO THE LORD** written upon the flower of life, upon that which is best, upon our intellect, upon our character, is to have it written everywhere; for here it must affect the labours of our hands, here it must influence the utterance of our lips, here it must control the path of our feet, here it must sweeten the influence we radiate". C. W. Slemming, **These Are The Garments,** pp. 163-164.

13. Anyone who hopes to see God must purify himself just as God is pure. 1 John 3:2,3.

14. We are reconciled in Christ (by what is in Christ) for the purpose of making us holy. Colossians 1:22,23.

15. Our uncleanness is opposite to God's holiness; thus the holiness we should have is freedom from sin. Isaiah 6:3,5; 1 Thessalonians 4:7; Isaiah 35:8.

16. Holiness is opposite to iniquity, and this is the point God want for us. Romans 6:19.

17. The new man given to us has holiness. Ephesians 4:24.

18. The unblameable heart is a holy heart. 1 Thessalonians 3:13.

19. Holiness is maintenance of freedom from sin. Romans 6:22.

20. The Holiness That God wants us to have is inner cleansing and works cleansing from sin. 2 Corinthians 7:1.

21. The point is that holiness must be our behavior. Titus 2:3.

22. It is obedience that we are called to that brings holiness. Exodus 19:5,6.

23. We must sanctify ourselves in holiness. 2 Chronicles 31:18.

24. It is God's holiness that we must partake of. Hebrews 12:10.

25. Sanctification makes us holy. Leviticus 11:44,45; Leviticus 20:7,8.

26. We were called to be holy in all manner of living just like God. 1 Peter 1:15,16.

27. Holiness makes us offer up sacrifices acceptable unto God. 1 Peter 2:5.

28. Holiness must be our reasonable/logical service. Romans 12:1.

29. We shall only see God if we have holiness. Hebrews 12:14.

30. Holy people are the redeemed of the Lord. Isaiah 62:12.

31. Those who come up in the first resurrection are holy. Revelation 20:6.

32. The real point is a new creature. 2 Corinthians 5:17; Galatians 6:15.

33. Look at these next points:

   a. **SALVATION:** DELIVRANCE FROM WRATH/DEATH FOR SINS, OR IS IT:

   b. **SALVATION:** HOLINESS TO THE LORD A NEW CREATURE.

INVESTIGATIONS INTO THREE ANTINOMIAN STATEMENTS

1. There are three types of knowledge, or knowledge is given in three different ways:

    a. **Direct knowledge**: This is the knowledge that is already formulated and communicated either by voice or by writing. Proverbs 22:20,21.

    b. **Derived knowledge**: This is knowledge that is not yet formulated, but is formulated by the observer from already existing realities. 1 John 3:16; Acts 23:6.

    c. **Implied knowledge**: This is knowledge that is implied but not stated in statements. Knowledge that is given at an implicative logical level; it is unstated but is sometimes discerned subconsciously and usually works out in the unconscious. John 14:6; Revelation 22:14.

2. We are now going to look at three antinomian statements from the point of view of implied knowledge. They are:

    a. The Law is abolished, we have love now.

    b. We are not under the Old Covenant Law; we are under the New Covenant.

    c. We are under Grace and not under the Law.

3. Let us look at the first antinomian statement in the light of **Implied knowledge**. If the Law is abolished and we have love now then:

    a. Love replaces the Law.

    b. As we had Law in the Old Testament we did not have love then.

    c. Love is different from the Law.

    d. Love is opposed to the Law.

    e. We can have love and transgress the Law, because there is no Law to in fact transgress.

4. But the real facts are love is not presented in the Bible as a replacement to the Law.

    a. Love exists in the First Witness or Old Testament. (Deuteronomy 7:7,8; Hosea 3:1); (Leviticus 19:18; Deuteronomy 6:5).

    b. Love is presented with the law in the F. W. or O. T. Exodus 20:6; Deuteronomy 10:12,13.

    c. Love is actually fulfilling the Law. Romans 13:8-10.

    d. If we have love we keep the Law. 1 John 5:2,3; John. 15:10; John 14:21,15.

5. No **Direct knowledge** or **Derived knowledge** teaches the above assumptions; there are no factual statements from which to derive the mythical points.

6. If we are not under the Old Covenant Law but under the New Covenant, then:

    a. The Old Covenant Law is against the New Covenant.

    b. The New Covenant was not in existence in the time of the Old Covenant.

    c. The New Covenant does away with the Old Covenant.

7. But the Bible reveals that:

    a. The New Covenant is the Law in the heart. Hebrews 8:8-12.

    b. The New Covenant existed in the Old Testament time of the Old Covenant. Psalm 37:30,31; Psalm 40:8; Isaiah 51:7.

    c. The Old Covenant is the Ceremonial Law. Hebrews 10:1-9,14-16.

    d. Thus it is wrong to present obedience to the Law, the Moral Law as the Old Covenant. 1 Corinthians 7:19; James 2:8-12; Revelation 14:12.

8. If we are under Grace and not under the Law then that would mean:

a. Grace is against the Law.

b. In the time of the Law there was no Grace.

c. One could have Grace and transgress the Law.

d. Grace saves us in transgression of the Law.

9. But Scripture teaches:

a. In the Old Testament there was Grace. Genesis 6:8; Exodus 33:12,13; Psalm 45:2; Psalm 84:11; Proverbs 3:33,34.

b. Grace saves us from transgression of the Law. (Ephesians 2:5,8; John 1:17; Matthew 1:21).

c. Grace establishes the Law. (Romans 4:5,16; Romans 3:31).

d. Obedience to the Law maintains the "under Grace" experience. Romans 6:14-17.

e. Grace and the Law aid each other. (Ephesians 2:8; 1 Corinthians 15:10; 1 Thessalonians 1:3; Hebrews 6:10; Romans 13:8-10); Psalm 119:29.

f. No Law means, no sin, hence no need of Grace. Romans 4:15.

APPENDIX

10. Translation of John 1:17. "Because the Law through Moses was given, the Grace and the Truth through Jesus came to be".

a. The Law is the writing of Moses. Matthew 22:36-40; Luke 2:22; Luke 24:44; John 1:45; John 8:5.

b. Moses being given the Law. Malachi 4:4; (Exodus 19:20; Exodus 20:21,22; Exodus 21:1; Exodus 24:3,4).

c. But since Moses was honored above Christ by the Jews. John 5:45-47; John 9:28,29.

d. The Grace and the Truth always came through Jesus Christ. (Revelation 13:8; Zechariah 4:7; Psalm 45:1,2).

e. Thus Christ was always greater than Moses. Hebrews 3:1-6.

f. Thus John is saying that all Moses gave were writings, but it was Jesus that always gave Grace and Truth (even in Moses' time). Jesus   is the Truth (John 14:6), Grace is from Him. Acts 15:11; 2 Corinthians 8:9; 2 Timothy 2:1.

THE END.

FALSE BABYLONIAN PENAL SUBSTITUTION AS OPPOSED TO BIBLICAL SUBJECTIVE SUBSTITUTION

1. The false Evangelical idea of penal-substitution.

> a. "In the case of the sin-offerings, the offerer came to the door of the tabernacle to give his life as the penalty for his sin, and there, having identified the victim with himself by laying his hand upon its head, the death of the sacrifice was accepted instead of his own. And this is what we understand by substitution, the sinner laid his sin upon the animal, and the victim died instead of him." Sir Robert Anderson, **The Gospel and its Ministry**, pp. 89-90.

2. The ancient Babylonian idea of substitution.

> a. "This was precisely one of the essential postulates of exorcism: it was thought, in fact, that evil, either actual or promised and predicted, could be transferred from one individual to another, and could in some way shift its weight—as with a burden. Among the innumerable exorcisms that have been preserved, and that evidence a universal and continuous practice, and a profound belief, whether they are very short ceremonies or long and solemn liturgies, this transfer of evil played a major role.

The sine qua non of its success seems to have been a close bond between the starting and finishing points of the "evil" in question, between the first bearer and the one on whom the evil was loaded. This bond could be either by contact, or by resemblance, with a frequent combination of the two. Often it was possible to be satisfied with some material object that was considered "to take" the evil (like a contagious disease). In a letter from Mari dating to around 1770 we have the oldest evidence of the knowledge of such an infection, of disease that is caught after the immediate contact with the "sick person". Very often figurines (salmu) in clay, in dough, in wax, in tallow, or in wood were used for that purpose. This had the advantage of being able to represent, more or less accurately, either an enemy to whom one wanted to pass on the evil one suffered, or another carrier who could even be the bearer of the evil himself, if needed." Jean Bottero, **Mesopotamia**, p. 142.

"When the threat was especially serious, for instance when it involved the life itself of the interested party, an animal could serve as substitute. We have a fragment of a ritual intended to ward off the death promised to someone, and entitled: In order to (procure) for Ereskigal (the queen of the dead) a substitute (puhu) of the interested party. It should be said in passing that we know that this ritual had been performed several times in the circle of Esarhaddon and Assurbanipal (ABL 439/140: 14; and 1397/299 rev.: 5). Here is a summary of the text; it is instructive and suitable for making us understand clearly both its functioning and especially

the spirit that inspired it. The sick person had to take with him to bed at night a small "virgin" goat. The next day a ditch with the outlines of a tomb was dug, and in it the sick person had to stretch out, still with his small goat. After that, the gestures of cutting the throat of both of them were made, with the difference that for the man a wooden blade was used, which did not hurt him, while for the animal a metal blade was used to cut its throat.

Then the small corpse was treated, as the human remains would have been. It was washed and perfumed, it was dressed in pieces of the clothes taken from the "diseased" person, and the officiating priest started the period of mourning by reciting a prayer and by proclaiming, as if it involved the "diseased": Behold the dead one! Then he organized a triple sacrificial funerary meal (kispu) in honor of Ereskigal, who had to be appeased, and for the commemoration of the spirits of the family of the person involved, as if a new deceased had joined their ranks. All that remained was to place the corpse ceremoniously in a shroud and to hold mourning for a decent period of time. The ill person had nothing to fear anymore because a living creature, identified with him both by contact (the night spent together) and by assimilation (the simultaneous cutting of the throat, the clothes of one placed on the other, the treatment of the corpse, the proclamation of death, etc.), had lost its life in his place.

Such a substitution was not an evasion or a way of leading the gods astray. The person just wanted to enable the gods to realize their wish, to accomplish their decision, under the same conditions but on another "basis" as close as possible to the one they originally had in mind, even if it was materially different. Similarly in law it was acceptable that a member of the immediate family of the debtor settles the debt in his place, and work as his substitute in the service of the creditor. That was the idea that the ancient Mesopotamians had about substitution and its role." **Ibid.**, p. 143.

3. While the word "substitute" is not in the Bible, the essential idea is there.

    a.   It is there in the sense of justice for wrong. Deut. 19:15-21.

4. But in the doctrine of salvation it is not seen as death in place of death. The word "anti" is not so used in the Bible.

    a. *"If that death on Calvary be indeed the payment of His people's debt, how can forgiveness now be preached as being of grace? Is it not a matter of the strictest justice, that they whose discharge was nailed to the Cross of Christ nineteen centuries ago, should, at the earliest moment possible, be set free? How can it be honest, or true, or right, to urge men to flee from the wrath to come, seeing that for some all wrath has been already borne, and the infliction of it now would be and outrage upon justice, and that for the rest there is no refuge open?"* Sir Robert Anderson, **The Gospel and its Ministry**, p. 87.

"It will therefore be here my aim to show that all such difficulties spring, not from the gospel itself, nor from the teaching of Holy Writ, but solely from forms of expression, and modes of thought, about the death of Christ, which are unwarranted by Scripture." **Ibid.**, p. 88.

"But, it will be urged, if Christ did not die as our substitute, salvation is impossible; and if He did so die for us, this fact must date from Calvary, and not from our conversion. This assumes that the death of Christ was instead of some, in such a sense as to make their salvation forensically a necessity, and that the salvation of any besides is a moral impossibility. Such difficulties only prove the danger of departing from the strict accuracy of scriptural expressions in dealing with these truths. To speak of Christ's dying instead of us, or as our substitute, is to adopt the language of theology, not of Scripture, and we must take care lest we use the words in a sense or a connection inconsistent with the truth. The teaching of Scripture is that he died for sinners (there is no emphasis on the preposition).

The language of ancient ancient Greece is far richer than our own in prepositions, and "instead of" has unequivocal correlative; but this word, though freely used by the LXX. (Anti) and found in the New Testament is never employed in such passages as Rom. 5:6,7,8. The statement of Matt. 20:28, repeated in Mk. 10:45, will not be considered an exception to this by anyone who marks the form and purpose of the text. The word (Huper) no doubt may have the same force, just as "for" in English. But in either case such a meaning is exceptional and forced; and in our own language we should in that case pronounce the word with emphasis, and print it in italics. A full and careful consideration of every passage where the word occurs will satisfy the student that it is never so used in the New Testament. The only text in which our translators have thus rendered it (2 Cor. 5:20) is a signal proof of this. An ambassador speaks on behalf of, not in the stead of, the court which accredits him. I need not say that substitution is an extra-scriptural expression." **Ibid.**, pp. 94-95.

"But to speak of the death of Christ as having this substitutional relationship to the sinner, apart from the change which takes place on his believing; and thus to make his pardon appear to be an act of justice in such a sense that it ceases to be an act of grace, is wholly unwarranted and false...But if the death of Christ be substitutionally instead of the unbeliever, his conversion may alter his condition spiritually and morally, but it can in no wise affect his judicial state: he is saved in fact and of right, whether he believes or not. In either case, grace is in chains, and not enthroned." **Ibid.**, pp. 97-98.

"Substitution, then is merely a theological statement of one aspect of this scriptural truth of the believer's oneness with Christ, and if it be taught apart from that truth, it may degenerate into error." **Ibid.**, p. 100.

5. However, the Bible does teach substitution in a subjective way. Matthew 20:28.

    a. We are dead in sins. Ephesians 2:1,5.

    b. Christ came that we might have life. John 10:10,11.

    c. Life is a substitute for death. Ephesians 2:1,5.

6. Many of the scriptures that teach salvific change have substitution in a subjective way.

    a. Circumcision removes the evil heart and substitutes love. Deut. 10:12-17.

    b. Another man, another heart in place of the former. 1 Samuel 10:6,9.

    c. The sick and sinful heart is replaced by a clean and white experience. Isaiah 1:5,6,16,18.

    d. A new heart substitutes the stony heart. Ezekiel 11:19,20.

    e. A new heart for the old one. Ezekiel 36:25-27.

    f. Born of the flesh is replaced by born of the Spirit. John 3:5,6.

    g. Death is substituted by life. Romans 5:17,21.

h. Death of the old man, new life is in its place. Romans 6:6-11.

i. The law of sin and death substituted by the law of the Spirit of life. Romans 8:1,2.

j. Sin in the flesh is replaced by the Righteousness of the law. Romans 8:3,4.

k. Minding the flesh is replaced by minding the Spirit. Romans 8:5.

l. Death- the carnal mind- is replaced by life-the Spiritual mind. Romans 8:6.

m. In the flesh is substituted by in the Spirit. Romans 8:8,9.

n. Old leaven is replaced by new leaven. 1 Corinthians 5:7,8.

o. Crucified replaced by being alive with Christ within. Galatians 2:20.

p. The Spirit replaces the flesh. Galatians 5:16,17.

q. Aliens without God, citizens with Christ. Ephesians 2:11-17.

r. The old man and his ways are replaced by the new man and his ways. Ephesians 4:17-24.

s. The powers of darkness to the kingdom of Christ. Colossians 1:13.

t. Was alienated but now reconciled. Colossians 1:21.

u. Dead in sins to be raised in life. Colossians 2:11-13.

v. The old man is gone, now the new man exists. Colossians 3:9,10.

THE END

DOES GOD DEAL WITH CONDEMNATION FIRST, OR WITH THE MORAL STATE IN MAN, WHICH?

1. Most religions present Justification as dealing with condemnation first. See:

> a. *"The teacher takes the belt. "Crack!" goes the belt. "Crack!" again and again. Welts rise up on John's back. Five, six. Blood spurts. Seven, eight, nine, 10,11. Mr. Primble has to look away. Twelve, 13, 14,15. And it is finished. John, all lacerated and bleeding, straightens up. Blood is running down his back. Now little Timmy turns around and as he sees the blood, tears stream down his face. He throws his arms around John and he hugs John and he says, "Oh, John—I'll love you forever!"*
>
> *That's the gospel, saved by our substitute meeting the demands of the law for us. And the result of the gospel is a heart broken in love. A heart that will love God and all the souls He died for, forever. So, you see, there is a difference between justification and sanctification. Justification saves us. Sanctification changes us. Justification is our ticket to eternal life. Sanctification is the proof that we have accepted the ticket and are on board. But always remember that your peace with God and your assurance of eternal life is in what Jesus did for you, not what you do for Him."* Steve Marshall, **What's The Difference?** P. 37-38.

b. "Because of His death on the cross, Christ's people are justified (freed from the condemnation of sin) in this life and shall be glorified (freed from the presence and influence of sin) in the life to come...Just as Christ died once to sin (i.e., to its guilt) and now lives to God, so the believer, must consider (reckon) himself dead to sin and alive to God "in Christ"...Only by realizing that he is dead to the condemning power of sin and alive to God "in Christ" can a sinner truly love or trust God." **Romans, an Interpretive Outline**, p. 48.

"These expressions mean that believers, through their identification with Christ, are dead to the GUILT of sin. They are viewed by God as If they themselves died in the death of Christ and suffered the full penalty of sin's guilt. Sin can no longer make any legal claim on them; thus, they are dead to it- free from its condemnation. That believers are not dead to the influence or power of sin in their lives is proved both by the Bible...and Christian experience...It exclusively indicates the justification of believers, and their freedom from the guilt of sin, having no allusion to their sanctification, which, however, as the Apostle immediately proceeds to prove necessarily follows." **Ibid.**,p. 46.

"The old view advocated by the Reformers and Puritans, failed by making the whole [dying to sin] too much a subjective experience, or an inward renovation. The origin of the misinterpretation must

be traced to the separation of the sixth chapter from the fifth, as if
a wholly new subject began at Rom. 6:1...To be 'dead to sin' is a
judicial or legal, not a moral figure. It refers to our release from
condemnation, our righteous disjunction from the claim and curse
of law." **Ibid.,**p. 47.*

2. Man has sinned and fallen short. Romans 3:23

3. We are thus all condemned. John 3:18,19.

4. Man has an evil heart. Jeremiah 17:9.

5. He transgresses God's law. James 2:8-12.

6. Man needs Justification. Romans 5:18.

7. But why does God need to deal with condemnation first? Possible answers:

   a. Since man is condemned he cannot receive God's love.

   b. Since God has condemned man He cannot give man His love.

   c. Therefore he must first free man or save him from condemnation, then man can receive love, or God could give him love.

   d. God must first accept the man before He can bestow His love on the man.

8. These theories are all wrong for various reasons:

   a. Man's real problem is not condemnation; it is the carnal mind. Genesis 6:5; Romans 8:6-8.

   b. For man to respond to God's love, God must first love man, thus we can receive love. 1 John 4:19.

   c. God gives us love while we are yet sinners. Romans 5:8; 1 John 3:16.

   d. God justifies the ungodly. Romans 4:5.

   e. Jesus prescribes internal cleansing first. Matthew 23:25,26.

9. Condemnation for the Carnal mind goes when internal change comes first. Romans 8:1-4.

10. Condemnation for past sins goes when the past sins are removed in the Judgment.

   a. Matthew 12:36,37.

   b. James 5:19,20.

   c. Revelation 20:11-15.

   d. John 5:24.

FORGIVENESS INVOLVES SELF-DENIAL OR THE LOSS OF SOMETHING TO THE FORGIVER.

1. Man is a sinner. Romans 3:10-19.

2. He is a sinner against God. Psalm 51:4.

3. God has wrath for sin. Romans 1:18; Romans 2:5,6.

4. This condemnation of wrath for sin is upon all. John 3:18,36.

5. Now if God must forgive us, He must do two things:

   a. Get rid of our sins. Psalm 103:12; Job 22:23.

   b. He must not punish us for sin. Ezekiel 18:23,4.

   c. But He is to remove sin first if He is to remove the punishment; because it is sin that has caused punishment, and once sin is existing, so will be punishment. Romans 6:23; Romans 5:12.

   d. Now, it is God Himself who punishes us. Isaiah 13:11; Hosea 4:9.

7. To forgive therefore, He Himself must turn from His urge to punish. Exodus 32:12,14; Jeremiah 26:19; Deuteronomy 13:17; Psalm 106:23.

8. What if God was to punish Christ the innocent and then tell us He forgives us if we repent. Here is this idea in this Evangelical book:

"God provided that the innocent could die for the guilty. The theologians call it vicariate; that is, done on the behalf of another. As we will later see, God illustrated this provision of substitution throughout all of the ritual sacrifices. He sought to establish in our minds that He was willing to accept the death of an innocent substitute as atoning for the sinner, providing he met certain qualifications. Only death could atone for sin; only death could eradicate the sin principle; only death could erase the marks of sin; and only death could satisfy God's law concerning sin. There could be no shortcut, no lowering of the price, no bartering with God. Death and only death can answer sin. But God offered to accept the death of an innocent substitute. If anyone could be found who was holy, harmless, unimpeachable, pure, and righteous, God offered to accept the shedding of his blood instead of the blood of the sinful one." Judson Cornwall, **Let us Enjoy Forgiveness**, p. 47.

"So although God has offered to accept the death of the innocent, there is no innocent one to be found in the world...For God took the sinless Christ and poured into him our sins. Then, in exchange, he poured God's goodness into us! Christ became the guilty, and we became the innocent..." **Ibid.**, p. 48.

"Calvary was a tremendous price to pay for sin, especially for an innocent victim, but Jesus paid it all... 'It is finished,' He cried, and at that moment every price that God would ever extract for sin, every penalty that could ever be levied for violation of God's law, and every cent that was owed because of sin was paid in full. As

Forgiveness Involves Self-Denial Or The Loss Of Something

Christ hung His head and died in the midst of darkness and anguish, sin's bondage was broken, sin's control over men was wrested away, and sin's power was negated. Sin became a caged, toothless lion, totally harmless if we stay outside the cage. The entire plan of redemption was finished. What God had planned, He had now performed. Men could now be fully forgiven because the price had been payed." **Ibid.**, p. 49-50.

"*The pardon does not make the man guiltless; it simply revokes the penalty of the law and releases the man. Forgiveness is not pardon in this sense. God will not – indeed He cannot—revoke the penalty of His law. He cannot, out of sheer magnanimity, set the condemned man free, as Pilate released Barabbas to the crowd... But while He cannot overlook sin, He can accept Christ's death as atoning for our sin and forgive that sin. Forgiveness deals with the sin; pardon, with the punishment."* **Ibid.**, p. 79.

"*We know, of course, that the blood answers to the penalty of sin. It is substitutionary atonement; that is, an innocent dies for the guilty, thereby satisfying the penalty of the law."* **Ibid.**, p. 127.

9. This would mean the following points:

    a.   He still did not let go of His wrath thus someone else had to take it, even the innocent.

b. This could only mean that, He, being **set** to punish was to the point of being unjust, since He punished the innocent in our place.

c. Thus what is being offered to us is not genuine forgiveness, for God did not turn from His fierce anger, He merely found a way to channel it, gratify it, and satisfy Himself.

10. This theory makes god's wrath a problem to Him, because He could not forget or lay this wrath aside and forgive us (and also change us), He had to gratify it, thus some writers represent God as being reconciled to us also.

a. *"Reconciliation—the answer to God's alienation from us."* Charles M. Horn, **The Doctrine of Salvation**, p., 28.

"This refers to the adjustment of differences by the removal of enmity and separation. There is practical unanimity among scholars that reconciliation in St. Paul mean a change of relation on God's part towards man, something done by God for man, which has modified what would otherwise have been His attitude to the sinner. Thus, reconciliation is much more than a change of feeling on man's part towards God, and must imply first of all a change of relation in God towards man." **Ibid.**, p. 31.

"Although the major idea of "enemies" in the context is that men were hostile to God, it also implies a strong reaction on God's part to man's sin. "Seen, then, in the wider context of the New

Forgiveness Involves Self-Denial Or The Loss Of Something

Testament thought, Rom. 5:8-11 may be said to indicate a reconciliation in which there is a Godward as well as a manward aspect."

The meaning of the Greek term would seem to indicate that the work of reconciliation itself has to do with the removal of God's enmity toward fallen man; whereas the change in man's attitude toward God is a result of reconciliation.

Note Godet's comments on this matter:

> *"Does this word denote man's enmity to God, or that of God to man? Hating God (dei osores) or hatred of God (Deo odiosi)? The first notion would evidently be insufficient in the context. The enmity must above all belong to Him to whom wrath is attributed; and the blood of Christ, through which we have been justified, did not flow in the first place to work a change in our disposition Godward, but to bring about a change in God's conduct toward us...In our passage the true meaning does not seem to us doubtful. The word being reconciled reproducing the being justified of ver. 9, it follows from this parallelism that it is God, and not man, who gives up His enmity. In the same way as by justification God effaces all condemnation, so by reconciliation He ceases from His wrath."*
> **Ibid.**, p. 32.

11. The real problems with this idea of the meaning of the death of Christ are the following points:

    a. Why must God punish Christ in our place, or instead of us, except He must relieve Himself of His wrath.

    b. Some mystical law or justice seem to prevent God from turning from His wrath, thus He must punish come what may.

    c. If He gratified His wrath, then He really has not turned from it or forgiven us.

    d. No self-denial (of practicing wrath) has been exercised by God; He still gratified His wrath.

12. To represent this schema, as God's love provision is grossly misleading. It is mere window dressing to say that: "God in His love provided this way of salvation, or give His Son to save us."

> a. *"It is entirely against all Pauline thought to think of Jesus Christ pacifying an angry God, or to think that in some way God's wrath was turned to love, and God's judgment was turned to mercy, because of something which Jesus did. The prime purpose of forgiveness is the restoration of a lost relationship. We have been forgiven so we can change our attitude from defensive anger to submissive love. We have been reconciled (made friendly, restored to fellowship) by God's outstanding demonstration of His consistent love, and Christ at Calvary is the apex of that manifestation."* Judson Cornwall, **Let Us Enjoy Forgiveness**, p. 80-81.

"Reconciliation is directed to the need created by God's alienation from us. It presupposes disrupted relations between God and men, an alienation, which on our part is caused by sin...This refers to the adjustment of differences by the removal of enmity and separation. There is practical unanimity among scholars that reconciliation in St. Paul mean a change of relation on God's part towards man, something done by God for man, which has modified what would otherwise have been His attitude to the sinner. Thus, reconciliation is much more than a change of feeling on man's part towards God, and must imply first of all a change of relation in God towards man.

Charles M. Horne, **The Doctrine of Salvation**, p. 30-31.

13. The real facts about that schema can be seen:

   a. God lost nothing, not even His Son, He has Him still.

   b. We may escape penalty by this plan, but God is the real winner (not man at all), because we could still be lost and fall under His wrath again, and He has already gotten the chance to gratify His wrath before.

14. Real forgiveness entails voluntarily giving up the right to punish, so if God satisfied it on Christ He hasn't really forgiven us. Numbers 14:11-20; 2 Chronicles 29:10; 2 Chronicles 30:6,8,9.

15. But here is the real Biblical idea of forgiveness in our salvation.

   a. Christ's death brings to light sufferings for sin. Hebrews 13:12; 1 Peter 3:18.

b. His death brings to light the gift of life. Matthew 20:28.

c. If we repent and believe, God will change our sinful hearts to a clean heart. Ezekiel 36:26,27; Psalm 51:10.

d. Thus God does not condemn us for that. Romans 8:1.

e. He makes us live holy and overcome sin. 1 John 1:7.

f. Then, in the Judgment, if we have kept His Law (lived holy), He forgives us for all our past sin (the condemnation for them). (1 John 4:16,17; 1 Peter 4:8); James 5:19,20.

16. This Plan represents God as turning from His wrath, or forgetting it on condition of reformation. Ezekiel 18:21-23,27-32.

THE END

INDEX

ABOUT THE AUTHOR

Brother NYRON MEDINA is a modern day Christian Reformer and founding Minister of the Thusia Seventh day Adventist Church in Trinidad and Tobago and its sister churches globally. He was used by YHWH God since the early 1980s to rediscover the authentic understanding of the Gospel as taught by earlier reformers such as German Martin Luther.

His discipline over the years in learning spiritual truths in the school of Christ has provided great leadership as the repairer of the breach that had been caused by years of apostasy from original Seventh day Adventism and ancient Apostolic Christianity. His leadership has also served as the restorer of the paths to dwell in, linking us today like a golden chain back to the retrieval of the pure biblical truths of the Gospel of Jesus Christ. No other contemporary Theologian has so accurately recaptured the Gospel, making our church the inheritors of the Reformation and establishing Brother Medina's rightful place in the line of Reformers since the 16th century.

Brother Medina is a prolific writer of Christian religious books, booklets and tracts, long time host and producer with his wife Sis. Dell Medina, of the Television and Radio programs "Escape for thy Life" which are aired in Trinidad and Tobago and St. Vincent and the Grenadines in the Southern and Eastern Caribbean respectively.

To contact this author call the number **1-868-373-6108**. To learn more about the Thusia Seventh day Adventist Church and receive our **FREE** religious booklets, tracts, video and audio bible studies, call **1-868-625-0446** or visit our website at www.thusiasdaevangel.com. You may also visit our Church's YouTube channel at **Thusia SDA Gospel**. May God bless you with sinfreeness as you study His words in these last days.

OTHER PUBLICATIONS BY THE AUTHOR

1. An Exposition of Revelation Chapter 13

2. Systematic Theology: The Seven Pillars, The Plan of Salvation

3. The Issue of the Covenants

4. Studies in Pantheism Part 1

5. Studies in Pantheism Part 2

6. Reformation Studies

7. Lucifertheism

8. Studies in Faith

Please contact the Thusia Seventh Day Adventist Church at Telephone number **1-868-625-0446** for further information on these and other publications.

NOTES

NOTES

Made in the USA
Middletown, DE
18 September 2022

10702623R00136